PENGUIN BOOKS
NARRATIVES:
THE STORIES THAT HOLD WOMEN BACK AT WORK

Mette Johansson (MBA, CSP, PCC) is a highly awarded author, speaker and consultant. She worked in leadership roles for multinational corporations for fifteen years before founding MetaMind, a training consultancy providing consulting and learning programmes in the people side of leadership skills.

Mette has spoken internationally on authentic, inspirational and inclusive leadership at a wide variety of global conferences, corporations and business schools. Her clients include Citibank, Airbnb, Microsoft, UPS, Pfizer, CapitaLand, and many more. Awards for her activities include the AmCham HERo award, the Asia Women Icon Award, HRM Asia Silver and Bronze, the Golden Door–REX Karmaveer Medal, and APAC insider's Best Leadership Development Company 2020 and 2022.

Mette is also the founder and relentless driver of the non-profit KeyNote–Women Speakers' directory, with a mission to bring diversity to speaking stages around the world. She is regularly featured in media in Singapore, from *Harper's Bazaar* to *The Straits Times*.

Having lived in ten countries outside her birthplace, Denmark, Mette is a global citizen who speaks fluently in four languages and currently calls Singapore home.

Narratives:
The Stories that Hold
Women Back at Work

Mette Johansson

PENGUIN BOOKS

An imprint of Penguin Random House

PENGUIN BOOKS

USA | Canada | UK | Ireland | Australia
New Zealand | India | South Africa | China | Southeast Asia

Penguin Books is part of the Penguin Random House group of companies
whose addresses can be found at global.penguinrandomhouse.com

Published by Penguin Random House SEA Pte Ltd
9, Changi South Street 3, Level 08-01,
Singapore 486361

First published in Penguin Books by Penguin Random House SEA 2023
Copyright © Mette Johansson 2023

ISBN 9789815144079

Typeset in Garamond by MAP Systems, Bengaluru, India

www.penguin.sg

Contents

Introduction

We think of ourselves as rational beings, but we still tend to believe all manner of myths. When we're accustomed to believing that something is true, we often don't question the facts, even when what we accept as truth is filled with obvious contradictions.

Here's one example that you might have come across: Actual words make up just 7 per cent of our communication with each other, while body language and tone of voice account for, respectively, 55 per cent and 38 per cent. You might even have quoted these figures.

A quick internet search provides a long list of sources that quote the theory as I have just done. So, isn't it true? Well, the numbers are based on research by Professor Albert Mehrabian, a noted psychologist who is a specialist in nonverbal communication. But the professor himself has noted that people often misrepresent or misinterpret his findings. Let's use common sense to dive deeper into these figures.

How would you invite someone out to lunch by using only body language or only tone of voice? If Mehrabian's theory, as it's repeatedly quoted, is right, we'd find it almost eight times easier to use only body language to communicate, since it accounts for 55 per cent of communication, versus the 7 per cent that words account for. And wouldn't it be more than five times easier to use just our tone of voice? Tone of voice accounts for 38 per cent of communication.

Now, trying to invite someone out with both tone of voice and body language but no words should give you 93 per cent of the total communication effect. It would become a complicated game of charades, wouldn't it? Wouldn't a quick written message with 'Would you join me for lunch on Friday?' i.e., the words that supposedly make up only 7 per cent of our message make it easier to settle the appointment?

The percentages don't make sense, do they? And still, I frequently hear this 7-55-38 rule of communication being cited.

The real story is, in fact, more nuanced. Professor Mehrabian was referring to our *feelings* about the person communicating. When the message, the vocal component, and the facial expression are incongruent, we trust the facial expression and voice much more than the message.[1] Think about someone who rolls their eyes and says, 'I trust you,' disdainfully. The message, voice, and body language are incongruent. In this case, we listen more than eight times as much to the body language and more than five times as much to the tone of voice than the words themselves. Now, that makes more sense, right?

Why don't we simply use our common sense to challenge Mehrabian's often (mis)quoted figures? After reading this, aren't you surprised that barely anyone steps back and questions the obvious logical fallacy in how Mehrabian's ratio is quoted?

According to a quote attributed to Albert Einstein, it's because 'common sense is the collection of prejudices acquired by age eighteen.'[2] That is, certain stereotypes and stories are deeply ingrained in society, and it takes a big effort to shatter those narratives.

Most of us aren't truly trained in critical thinking. In his celebrated book *Thinking, Fast and Slow*,[3] Daniel Kahneman writes that we aren't psychologically equipped to judge our own thinking when we hear arguments that fit nicely into our existing patterns of beliefs or prejudices.

As a result, harmful myths are perpetuated for generations, and the ones we focus on in this book are creating inequality and injustice. While diversity and inclusion issues go far beyond gender, in this book, I'll focus solely on narratives that negatively affect women. After all, women carry half the sky, as Mao Zedong is famous for saying; but we remain at a disadvantage in corporate life.

Only 10.4 per cent of Fortune 500 CEOs are female.[4] In the developed world, women do eleven hours more unpaid work every week than men. In the developing world, it's a whopping eighteen hours more.[5,6,7] And this inequality is partly due to false narratives that society tends to accept without questioning, just like we've accepted the myth about the importance of body language and tone.

It's high time to question these narratives that hold women back in the workplace.

Here's an example from my own personal experience from years ago, when this book had only been a mere concept.

One evening, when I was having drinks with some male executives after a meeting, the subject of the #MeToo movement arose. Several of the men mentioned that the #MeToo movement had gone 'way overboard' or 'too far'. And it is not the only time I've heard this. One of the executives claimed that many men had been 'falsely accused of sexual misconduct,' and a few others nodded in agreement. He added how 'horrible it is that so many men's careers are being ruined'.

How do you respond to that? There have been a few high-profile cases where executives or men in power have been falsely accused of unwanted advances or sexual misconduct, allegedly. But the reality is that these cases pale before a 'a wave of lawsuits and arbitrations filed' by women in the 1990s and 2000s on 'pay, promotion, and pregnancy discrimination and, in some cases explosive allegations of hostile work environments, rampant sexual harassment, and even rape'.[8]

This 'wave' is probably no surprise to most working women. In one study[9], 81 per cent of women said they had been sexually harassed during their lifetime.

Let me stress here that, of course, it's tragic when any man—or woman—is accused of a serious offence that they didn't commit. But if even half of the reported 81 per cent of women have, in fact, been sexually harassed, it's a far greater tragedy than the few men who have been falsely accused. When I went home to search for prominent cases after being told that #MeToo had gone 'way overboard' by the male executive, Google provided me with exactly two cases.

And it doesn't get better when working remotely. In 2020, within weeks of the lockdown at the beginning of the COVID-19 crisis, more than a third of women were found to have endured at least one sexist demand at work. For instance, while the general trend was to dress casually when working from home, some employers urged female employees to dress sexier for Zoom meetings.[10]

Can we really claim that the #MeToo movement has gone 'way overboard' when men usually find themselves employed after harassment cases, sometimes continuously so at the same company? On the contrary, after reporting sexual harassment, many women are forced to leave the company or leave voluntarily, finding the burden of staying too heavy. There are reports that even for people on Wall Street who speak up as witnesses for alleged victims, it's difficult to keep and find employment there.[11]

Why we believe the myths

When we take a step back and a take a minute to think about it rationally, none of this makes sense, so obviously, common sense is not that common. We aren't the rational beings we claim to be.

Instead, we misjudge tnarratives—such as '#MeToo has gone too far'—for a variety of reasons beyond 'thinking fast', which is what Kahneman calls our automatic, impulsive, and intuitive thinking that is based on subconscious knowledge. It's the thinking we apply that doesn't question myths such as the ones in this book and that can easily be dispelled when 'thinking slow', while questioning and seeking perspectives.

Meaning in addition to not applying common sense, there are various reasons why we believe in these narratives. First, we focus much more on stories that we can relate to directly, primarily because they affect someone like us. A white male banker relates more easily to a story about a white male banker because it's much closer to his life and circle—to what he knows. If someone like you is a victim of wrongdoing, their story will catch your attention much more than a story about two billion people who suffered some sort of harassment. (If two billion sounds like a wild exaggeration, think about it: Based on the 81 per cent of women on this planet who will experience sexual harassment or worse in their lives, it's a conservative extrapolation.)

As has often been quoted, 'A single death is a tragedy; a million deaths are a statistic.' Unfortunately, this is true. The human brain is persuaded by *emotional* stories. Newspapers have known this since their first issue was printed more than 2,000 years ago in Rome. Plus, incidents near us sell much better than stories from a faraway country. We're selfish without realizing it. We care more about our own country and neighbourhood than starving people and wars in distant regions.

Which brings us to the second point. As news editors also know, people in power shape the stories we read and see. Men have more power in the world than women, especially on Wall Street, where it wasn't until March 2021 that a giant, global entity like Citibank appointed its first female CEO, Jane Fraser.[12] Men have been—and still largely are—in power on Wall Street and control the narrative. Since other men can empathize with a man losing his job when innocent, the story is recounted, and it thrives.

Third, there remain many biases about women and cases that involve harassment and even rape, with phrases like, 'I think she wanted it,' 'Didn't she ask for it?', 'Look at how she was dressed!', or 'She's too ugly for anyone to touch her!' still being common.[13] At the same time, we give men more than the benefit of the doubt. The Adam and Eve narrative lingers, as we assume men are innocent, while women are 'temptresses'.

Fourth, we tend to attribute our successes to our hard work, talent, and maybe a little bit of luck, but not to inherent privilege.

It feels nicer when we think that we deserve our success. We aren't likely to attribute our success to a father with great connections. We're not likely to say, 'I sailed through the selection process because I'm a white man.' Those with such privilege start believing that they got the job or promotion because of merit. Yes, they are typically fully convinced that they deserve it. We take it for granted. And as a result, privilege becomes invisible to those who have it.

It can be very visible and real when you don't have it, though.

Fifth, in situations where the power dynamic is unequal and psychological safety is lacking, minority groups won't speak up for their own benefit because they fear repercussions. Whistle-blowers may face a backlash.

You can be a change agent

Of course, worst-case scenarios of sexual harassment and rape should be argued in court. Therefore, in the pages that follow, I primarily focus on the daily issues that women face in the workplace—issues that you're able to question and that you're able to raise your voice about to effect change.

It's my aim to increase awareness about the myths being told in many companies by providing facts, stories, and arguments that shatter these narratives. I have been privy to the widespread damage of these gender-based myths in action—during my corporate career, in my role as the founder and CEO of MetaMind, a leadership training consultancy, as well as being the founder and chair of KeyNote Women, a global non-profit community of women speakers that is on a mission to bring more diversity to the world's speaking stages.

I have focussed on women, and of course I know that this immediately can be an invitation for criticism. Yes, there are many narratives targeted at people from various ethnic groups, people of different abilities, and many other identity groups. And as I claim time and time again, inclusion is not like a menu where you can pick and choose what you want. Inclusion is an attitude to value and respect everyone, regardless of their backgrounds and identities. I have focussed on one specific topic because, going back to Mao Zedong, women do hold half the sky. This book includes stories from a wide variety of women.

We also know that there are more than two genders and that stereotyping can be very harmful. I have generalized in this book. While stereotypes are not universally valid, generalizing does, to a certain extent, help us understand how society typically works. Clustering differences helps in this process and the fact is that research does show differences between men and women. If we don't discuss and seek to understand these, we will not advance. Research refers mostly to two genders too, although we know that the world is more complicated than that. So, I will generalize and simplify in this book at times.

This leads me to one disclaimer. If I, at any point of time, write or say, 'women do this,' 'men think that'—please read 'many women may prefer . . .' and 'most men tend to . . .' It makes reading a lot more pleasant than if I were to be very politically correct every single time I refer to genders.

If you find it hard to believe that some of these narratives still persist—I'm happy. Companies and cultural contexts vary, and we all have different experiences. It means that your environment is more progressive than the environments that I, or those interviewed for the book, encountered. Feel free to skip the chapter, although you may also benefit from knowing that the narratives in this book are real—they are out there. I have only included stories that I have come across repeatedly. And I want to give everyone the opportunity to do their part in shattering the myths.

I have provided plenty of data and facts, but naturally, there is also interpretation and opinion in this book. Data is not always available or relevant in specific situations, to certain groups of people, or at differing points of time. If you disagree—that's fine. Feel free to skip a chapter and move to the next.

Towards that end, I have divided this book into two parts. The first part contains the myths themselves. At the end of the discussion of each myth, I provide arguments that you can use in your world to begin to change the narrative. The second part of the book provides ten communication skills to help you make your arguments more convincing.

I urge you to keep the book at hand to consult whenever you encounter one of the myths. You can then refer to the relevant pages and use the arguments and skills to change the landscape wherever you are. If enough of us are armed with the facts, stories, and relevant communication skills, we can work together to collectively wipe out gender bias and inequality so that women and other disadvantaged groups can take their rightful place in the business world.

For you, your colleagues, your partners or wives, daughters, friends, acquaintances, and all minorities who are at a disadvantage in their careers, we must dispel these myths and create a more equitable work environment across the world.

Mette Johansson

Section I

Myth One

'Women Are Too Emotional'

'In India historically, we women are brought up to be subservient, suppress our own emotions and just comply. "Do as you're told,", "Play your role as a wife; it's your duty." We quickly learn to not express our feelings.' Married at age twenty, Lakshmi Murlidharan moved in with her in-laws and never expressed her wants, even though she had the urge to voice her opinions many a time.

'We get so used to the men in the house controlling our decisions and emotions. But you eventually burst at some point in time,' she told me. 'You start training your mind at a very young age to believe that emotions are bad, and if you show your emotions, you make yourself too vulnerable.'

Being a bit of a rebel at heart, Murlidharan decided to work to build her own identity. She chose to work in sales, a not-so-common career choice in India for women, since it comes with travel, which is considered less appropriate for women in many places around the world, and not least in India. But being in front of clients is what Murlidharan loves doing and excels at, and she is happy about her choice.

Throughout her career, she has repeatedly been asked, 'Why are you so emotional?' and has been told not to be. One year, while working for a large American HR service company in India, she didn't get the bonus she felt she deserved. The terms for the bonus were changed to be linked to the Asia-Pacific region's profitability. Having overachieved the target for the national market, she argued with her boss that not receiving the bonus was unfair. The word 'unfair' was the trigger for him. Her boss answered, 'Just don't get emotional about it. I can't do anything now. We'll see next year.'

'I *was* emotional,' Murlidharan says. 'I kept asking myself, "Why is this seen as emotional? Why can't I be emotional? What's wrong with being emotional? Does it make me any less professional?" I felt it was unfair to not be paid for the hard work I had put in and for the results the company benefitted from.' As a result of being treated unfairly, she left the company.

She also argued that being emotional is a strength in her job as a sales director. 'Emotions are core to selling,' she said. 'Selling is emotional. My sales success is linked to how I am emotionally connecting with my clients. It is linked to how much I care about their business and their challenges.' I'd urge you to take her word for it, since she regularly over-delivers on sales targets.

Reflecting on a colleague who is much more transactional in business dealings as well as in leading teams, Murlidharan says, 'I feel we need to put in emotions when it's about clients and the team. I do what I do for people. We're not playing chess, right? I am emotional. By being told I am too emotional, I feel guilty for having these emotions. So, I did some introspection. Why do I feel guilty showing emotions? The answer I found is that growing up, I was always made to understand to not show emotions. "Just comply." At work, I have been told that if I want to go up the career ladder, I'm not supposed to show emotions.'

Hearing a woman say she feels guilty for being emotional just confirmed to me the need for this book. Why don't we allow emotions at work? Think about it: What beings don't have emotions? Dead ones. Is that what we strive for at work—to be machines, or play chess, as Murlidharan said? Humans are social beings, and emotions are the glue that keeps us together.

Murlidharan went on to say, 'I rather want to have emotions than not care. Why is it called emotional when you're calling out things? I want to be in an organization that allows me to be the person I am. With passion, with emotions.'

Lakshmi Murlidharan, you deserve to be in an organization that allows you to be the person you are. Everyone deserves this.

Emotions can be superpowers

At a different time and place, Dalia Feldheim, the chief medical officer for Asia in a large multinational corporation, sat in her boss's office. She shared her frustration about a project that hadn't worked out the way she'd hoped. She had tears in her eyes, and her boss handed her a box of tissues. She noticed there was something strange about his smile. That's when he turned the box around to show her the handwritten post-it on it: 'Dalia's tissues.'

It was in stark contrast to the reaction of her earlier boss at Procter & Gamble. He had handed her a tissue box, too, and told her some very comforting words: 'Dalia, don't ever be embarrassed about your passion. It is not a weakness. Passion is your superpower.'

Her boss at Procter & Gamble is the one who was right. One scientific paper provides an extensive literary review of the effects of passion in the workplace. It cites studies which conclude that passion drives creativity, provides energy to perform better, motivates people to seek knowledge, makes work fun, and makes people more willing to go the extra mile to accomplish organizational tasks. It further describes passion as an energy mobilizer for enhancing organizational performance. It claims that passion has proved to act as a collaborator with purpose to enhance the performance of professionals.[14]

If we don't express feelings, we're probably supressing them. Why on earth would anyone want to suppress passion at the workplace when it has such big, positive implications on productivity?

Feldheim shared with me some advice that she'd received from another boss: Talk about emotions unemotionally. 'I never managed to do so, though,' she says with fervour. 'I am emotional. My emotions have a role. They mirror my feelings. I was passionate, and I delivered. I delivered the moon.' She has a point. Her marketing campaign 'Like A Girl' has seventy million views on YouTube[15], and the campaign resulted in a dozen advertising awards, including the industry's most prestigious ones—Cannes and Effie.

Feldheim confronted the boss who placed the post-it on the tissue box. His response? 'This is just boy bantering. Don't you have a sense of humour?' She reported the incident to HR, which reprimanded him, but there were no further repercussions during her employment there. In the end, Feldheim voted with her feet. She left the corporate world and now teaches, consults, writes, and speaks[16].

The penalty for women being labelled as emotional, as both Murlidharan and Feldheim experienced, is wide-ranging. Studies show that when a woman is told to 'calm down' during a disagreement, or when she is explicitly labelled as 'emotional', her argument is seen as significantly less legitimate[17].

Yes, women are seen as less competent when they are blamed for being emotional.

Boys don't cry, but they may slam the table

Feldheim pointed out to me that while a woman might leave a meeting room in an emotional state, 'Men leave the room in anger all the time.' Yes, men do demonstrate anger more frequently than women. The double bind is at play, which means women are 'Damned if they do and damned if they don't'—penalized for asserting themselves but ignored when they don't[18]. If a woman is too kind, she isn't a leader. If she gets just a little tougher, she's a cold, calculating b****.

The double bind means that as women leaders, they're held to a higher standard of competency and often reap smaller rewards than men. Research shows that it's difficult for women to be seen as both competent *and* likeable; they're seen as one or the other.

Women who express anger receive 'status penalties' relatively higher to men who express anger, according to various studies.[19] Plus, let's not forget that anger is an emotion.

When women express emotions in the workplace, we see it as their personality and usually ascribe it to a personality flaw. When men express emotions in the workplace, we see it as circumstantial. We might say, 'He got upset about the market downturn.' As a result, we typically sympathize with their emotions that result from challenges.

Of course, in cultures with a highly diverse mix of ethnicities, such as the US, there's a big difference in how the intersectionality or combination of gender and race play a role in our interpretations of expressed emotions. Research shows that Black women might not be penalized as harshly as white or Asian women for aggressive behaviour. At the same time, there's a prevailing stereotype that 'Black people are aggressive.' Even powerful women like Michelle Obama have been a victim of this myth. In a live interview with her, which I attended in Singapore, she shared how she has been labelled an 'angry Black woman' for simply having an opinion.

In general, women are expected to be 'nice'. Is this one of the reasons we tend to accuse women of being too emotional?

I often say that the rules in the business world, quite literally, have been written by the straight (or at least acting straight), able-bodied, white American man. Just look at the authors' names on the books that are taught at the world's top business schools. In my view, this is the reason why emotions that are more frequently demonstrated by men, such as anger, are seen as acceptable in the workplace, whereas those that are more frequently demonstrated by women are seen as 'unprofessional' and as best kept private.

'Professorssionalism'—in the eyes of the male-defined business world—apparently means toughening up and putting on a mask to hide our feelings, yet the Oxford Dictionary definition of professionalism is simply 'the high standard that you expect from a person who is well trained in a particular job'.[20]

And have you considered that humans don't cry just when they're sad? We also cry because we're happy, or as in Feldheim's case, frustrated. Tears have a bodily function and may play a therapeutic role. When we cry for emotional reasons, we're involved in a healing process.[21]

Emotions are information.[22] They help us understand how best to act in different situations. For instance, if we feel insecure and unwelcome, it is information that something is wrong. We can ask what the underlying reason is for feeling insecure and unwelcome, for instance, do people trust us? This again gives us the opportunity to design strategies to build trust. Reflecting on what's going on below the surface to understand our relationship is the first step to changing the situation.

Recognizing and owning our emotions not only makes us more emotionally intelligent but also healthier and more balanced. It's worrisome to consider that men are discouraged from expressing certain emotions from a young age , like 'Boys don't cry.' This wrong but, unfortunately, a central element of too many boys' upbringing may be the real problem. It means that boys are, all too often, deprived of the healing process that tears naturally provide. Of course, being brought up to believe that it is wrong to cry is exactly why men—and often enough people of all genders—don't see tears as professional. Society would be better off if both men and women were allowed to stay in touch with their emotions at all times, including at work.

The attitude of most cultures that 'Boys don't cry' isn't the only reason men shed tears less frequently than women—9 per cent versus 41 per cent, respectively.[23] From a very young age, women are discouraged from expressing frustration in ways that are considered fine for men, such as slamming a fist on a table or raising their voices. Instead, the outlet of choice for women when expressing frustration is often tears. There's also a biological explanation for why women cry more—they produce more prolactin, a hormone linked to producing tears.[24]

Feldheim realized that it may be difficult for others to deal with her emotions and said that it's important to describe to people what's going on for her when she becomes emotional. She isn't embarrassed by an occasional tear, and if others are, she asks them not to be, explaining that it's her way of expressing frustration.

Feldheim also shared tips with me on how to manage emotions, including taking a deep breath, centring your body, perhaps even leaving the room for a moment. In other words, take a step back to analyse the situation, deal with your feelings, and carefully consider your response. We can all benefit from working on managing our emotions.

The fact is that whether it's tears or laughter, empathy or excitement, women tend to express a range of emotions more frequently than men do, while men's emotional expression is, generally speaking, relegated to anger and some level of joy.

This may be a major contributor to negative sentiments against women as leaders. One out of eight Americans doubt women's emotional suitability for politics[25]. Only 47 per cent of people in the G20 are 'very comfortable' with having a woman as head of government—only 43 per cent of men and 52 per cent of women.[26] 10 per cent across the G20 say that they are not comfortable with a large company having a Jane rather than a John as a CEO. It gets worse in South Korea, where 29 per cent people don't feel comfortable with a female CEO.

It is quite ironic because the reason we mistrust women as leaders is probably that when emotional, we can't take the needed rational decisions—which is true for all genders (see p. 113 and 155). However, doesn't the anger that men demonstrate beat sadness or frustration as an obstacle for rational decision making? Acting in the heat of the moment, perhaps even seeking revenge, seems risky to me. The basis of this irrational narrative defies logic.

A British banker and a strong male ally shared his anger about men getting angry. 'I've seen men get very emotional all the time, but the emotions are anger, violence, domination, and it's hierarchical. Often men climb hierarchies via domination. And they expect you to be subservient. If you're subservient, they claim to "take care of you". If you are not subservient or if you call them out for making a mistake, squandering resources, or being foolish—even when done in a very reasonable way—they can get really, really angry with you because you're not supposed to call them out. And then they can go to that emotional place.'

'Their anger can rise in a period of a few seconds. It overwhelms them and they will be saying the most obscene things without realizing how obscene it is, because they are lost in anger,' he continued. He stressed that it rarely happens in a mixed gender environment, stressing the point that mixed gender workplaces are simply better.

'It's like a little scrap fight club when there are no women present. We men can just get at it. It's like men's little secret. And I've seen that old fashioned chivalry—gentlemen like—of not swearing because there are women on the call, and they may get upset.'

An interesting thought when you come to think of it—women will get upset about swearing at the office, and men will not.

Rashmi Dalai, an American expert associate partner in innovation and design at Bain & Company, told me over breakfast that the strongest emotion she experiences at the workplace is anger from men. 'Women are not allowed to express anger. But I'm often on the receiving end of it and I'm supposed to just accept it.'

'I have regular conversations with a friend where we wash out the microaggressions that I receive as a woman and frustrations about larger angry outbursts that men feel they are entitled to direct at you,' she says. 'They use aggression to reassert their domination over you,' is how she perceives it.

I observe with interest that both the British banker and Dalai have stated spontaneously that anger is used to reassert dominance over others. And while eating my yoghurt with fruits and granola in conversation with Dalai, I wonder how come any leaders in the twenty-first century still don't have the decency to treat colleagues with respect.

Convincing proof of persisting inequalities

Caroline Farberger, partner and chairwoman at Wellstreet, lived and made a career as a man until age fifty, which was when she went through gender affirming surgery. Who can be a better witness than Farberger for the different experiences we have in corporate life depending on our gender?

'What I didn't see was my privilege as a male to just be myself every day,' she said in a podcast with Die Boss (German play of word illustrating 'the female boss'). 'I could come to the office in whatever mood I was; happy, angry or whatever. And my authority would never be questioned.'

She confirmed that women's authority is questioned when they behave in the same way: '[Now] I realize that women in business have a narrower corridor of acceptable behaviours. Whereas men in my own experience have a much wider corridor of acceptable behaviours without risking losing their position or without risking losing their authority.'

She also confirmed that women are labelled as emotional when they miss that narrow corridor. She described how being too passionate is seen as negative, and you can't be too assertive, either—but you must take your place.

'I now much better understand why many women just don't have the energy to make it through,' says Farberger, who made it to the top when her identity papers still categorized her as male.

What emotions must we manage?

Do we want to express emotions or manage them?

Regardless of gender, this depends on their impact on others:

- **Angry outbursts**, when directed at individuals, can have considerable negative impact, such as fear, insecurity, avoidance, and stress. Paul Ekman, a pioneer in the study of emotions, claimed that anger is the most dangerous emotion.[27] I would thus argue that it is inappropriate to show anger in a professional environment.

- If we're **frustrated** or disappointed and share it with others, our feelings are less likely to have a negative impact on the other people in the room. My argument is therefore that unless it is directed at individuals, it is okay to show that you're human and that you are frustrated.

- **Passion**, when expressed through **enthusiasm**, can lead to inspiration and increased engagement, especially when it evokes passion in others. It does not just belong in a professional environment, it is a core leadership skill. Expressing pride about your team's work falls in the same category.

- **Empathy**[28] and **compassion** can heal the negative emotions of others. When we address someone's frustrations, wants, and needs, they feel **heard**. As a result, we gain their trust, loyalty, and engagement in return.

At the workplace, negative emotions are more frequently demonstrated by men. Other emotions are more frequently demonstrated by women[29]. Isn't it very obviously a myth that women's emotions are unprofessional? Why do we keep on reinforcing it, then?

Maybe those who say women are too emotional are the ones who should 'man up' and get used to the expression of a broader range of feelings.

EQ is an asset

'I've had male bosses who were very emotional,' Feldheim says. 'Creativity needs emotions. The Run Like a Girl campaign became so successful because the then creative director at Leo Burnett and I are very emotional and passionate.'

I agree. High emotional intelligence or EQ is 'the ability to recognize one's own and other people's emotions, to discriminate between different feelings and label them appropriately, and to use emotional information to guide thinking and behaviour.'[30] These are highly valuable skills in any professional setting. They weren't necessarily a century ago when manual labour was the main occupation we had. However, in a knowledge economy, we want our minds to work effectively. As we will see later, when emotions such as fear are at play, our rational thinking is switched off. Leaders must develop their emotional intelligence today.

Around the world, female leaders are showing more emotions, such as empathy. Take former New Zealand Prime Minister Jacinda Ardern, who famously consoled victims of the

Christchurch mosque shootings in 2019. Pictures went viral, since such an authentic demonstration of empathy, and that too towards people from a different faith, was uncommon.

Of course, there are also men who demonstrate empathy, such as former US President Barack Obama. In 2016, he hugged an elderly survivor of the Hiroshima nuclear bomb, allowing the expression of appropriate emotions to be viewed as an asset.

Being emotional is not just about being empathetic or comfortable with tears. Feeling inspired and showing our passion and pride in our work and our teams are other powerful expressions of emotion. We don't go to work to do a job these days. We want to pursue a calling, or, at the very least, contribute to a higher purpose.

Consider for a moment, yes, we may be inspired by someone who is doing an excellent job, perhaps even against all odds. Without the communication of it, without sharing it with others, it may go unnoticed. Isn't it when a person authentically demonstrates their passion for a topic, communicating the big picture enthusiastically with high energy, that we become the most inspired to join their mission?

Take some of the most famous speeches in the world such as the 'I have a dream' speech by Dr Martin Luther King Jr. More recently, I was highly impressed by the passionate speech of very high calibre from Ukrainian President Volodymyr Zelenskyy when Russian President Vladimir Putin began invading Ukraine in 2022.[31] In these instances, passion and emotion expressed by men are accepted. What would these speeches have been without passion?

A 2015 *Harvard Business Review* article told the story of a female executive, who found herself speaking loudly and gesturing with her hands for effect. The article describes how a male colleague sitting across from her waved his hand across his throat, gesturing like a movie director cutting a scene. He shut her down and redirected the conversation back to the product.[32]

The advice given by the article's authors was to avoid miscommunication by being intentional with passionate language with a moderate tone, along with facts and logic. May this be because the authors are accepting the male view and the presenter is female, and the advice is to suppress emotions at work? And is this really the advice we want to give people?

I usually argue very strongly for expressing your excitement and using effective body language. I coach leaders to show more enthusiasm and share their passion about their work to inspire others. Also, I work with close to a hundred different companies, and as an external speaker, I get away with showing enthusiasm and passion.

Of course, company cultures do differ. I interviewed a woman who works for a British company, where the work culture clearly doesn't appreciate enthusiasm in management meetings. When the English say, 'I was a bit disappointed that . . .' they likely mean 'I'm most upset and cross.'[33] English culture isn't known for the expression of passion—at least not until after a pint or two at the pub.

Of course, your use of emotions needs to be adapted to the culture—organizational and industry culture as well as country culture. Some cultures are more ready than others to drop the notion that we are only professional when we suppress all emotions. Your natural adaptation to cultures will hopefully ensure that when I ask you to embrace enthusiasm and passion, it is likely to be a step in the right direction for you—and not an over-the-top expression of inappropriate emotion.

The implications of calling a woman 'too emotional' are bigger than you may think

When we don't allow 50 per cent of the population to express feelings in a way that's natural to them, we're essentially telling them that they don't fully fit in. It may be one more hint as to why so many women find that the workplace isn't made for them.

As we have demonstrated, women more often display emotions that have positive overall effects on the organizations where they work. Yet, the belief that being 'emotional' is negative causes a reduction of opportunities for women to become leaders, even dismissing women as leadership material in general.

It's time that we start seeing passion and high emotional intelligence as assets rather than liabilities. We want empathetic leaders who understand us. We're inspired by leaders who show their passion and enthusiasm. So, let's promote more people who are able to do so!

How to counter the myth that women are too emotional

Note

Every narrative in this book is followed by statements, questions, and arguments to help you shatter that particular myth. You may choose the appropriate argument against the myth based on the situation, cultural customs, the person you are in conversation with, and your personal communication style.

Part two of the book goes into further detail with communication skills and strategies for any situations and circumstances.

When subjected to statements such as 'Women are too emotional,' or 'Women are too emotional to be leaders,' you can respond by saying:

- 'Do you think emotions are harmful?'
- 'What emotions are desirable, and which are undesirable at the workplace? Why are these emotions undesirable at the workplace?'

- 'High EQ—being able to access appropriate emotions— is an asset. Luckily, more and more organizations have come to realize this. When we're able to listen and act on our emotions, we are not only more balanced, happier, and building a strong and positive work culture, but productivity at the workplace increases, too.'
- 'I know that when I show emotions, it can be very beneficial. Emotions drive my passion, and passion allows me to do extraordinary things. Also, when I show my enthusiasm for my work, it inspires other people. And when I show my team how proud I am of what we've achieved together, their engagement is boosted.'
- Perhaps followed by: 'I use emotions strategically to increase productivity in my team.'
- 'How would you describe a man if he expressed this emotion?' (Note: This is more likely to work when passion is expressed, as opposed to tears.)
- 'If one of our senior male leaders would have demonstrated this behaviour, how do you think people would have described him?'
- 'Women are clearly held to higher standards. When women raise their voices, they're labelled "angry" and "hysterical". When men raise their voices, they're labelled "assertive", "passionate", and "driven".'

Myth Two

'We Adhere to Meritocracy'
Or 'We Take the Best Person for the Job'

'We've already looked at our hiring, appraisal, and promotion criteria and eliminated gender bias,' I was told over lunch by a female regional president of a Fortune 500 company based in Singapore.

A little further into our meal, she shared that women bring a lot of attributes and benefits to leadership that men don't. 'For instance, we are typically much more reflective,' she pointed out.

'Is this taken into account in your hiring, appraisal, and promotion criteria?' I asked.

After a brief pause, she answered, 'You've got me there.'

This is hardly an unusual situation. A female Pakistani chief human resources officer recently told me, 'I see that women bring some very different strengths to the table—for instance, patience. There is too much losing temper and raising voices going on in the boardroom. The company will benefit from more gender diversity.'

Even though she claimed the company was fully meritocracy-based, the conversation clearly showed that patience and civility were not on their list of necessary, or even desirable, talents during any of the people processes guiding hiring to firing. These are skills in which she knows women outperform men.

I see it regularly in companies that I work with. There is still a male lens to the behaviours that are rewarded in all people processes and the definitions of what constitutes good leadership.

The narrative of 'hiring the best person for the job' is the myth about adhering to meritocracy. Meritocracies purportedly choose 'the best person for the job', but how is that true when the criteria for merit are narrowly defined for a male workforce, typically dominated by one ethnicity? How can a company claim to be meritocracy-based when the essential skills in which women outperform men are not taken into consideration? It's glaringly obvious that like most others, this Pakistani company isn't truly hiring the best person. I suspect they may be hiring the best *man* for the job.

'We want diversity—meaning we want a woman, which I find a bit insulting. We want good people, right? In this case, we had defined clear criteria for hiring,' a faculty member at Penn State shared with me, 'but they were willing to put aside these criteria with a candidate because he came from a very prestigious university. They were closing their eyes to his lack of suitability to the position and were very lenient on him during the interview. In my interview with him, he didn't do a great job answering my questions.' Still, he was the recommended candidate.

'We have judgements inherently within us. We don't even know that we are discriminating. We think we are fair, but we are discriminating in every aspect. When it comes to men, we see them as good unless they prove they are bad. There are double standards,' she asserted.

Are countries truly meritocracies?

The US economy claims to be based on meritocracy, and just like in so many other aspects, plenty of companies around the world have followed the American school of thought—hiring as per society's traditionally defined leadership standards. So much for the 'land of opportunity' and 'the American dream', where anyone can supposedly make it if they try hard enough.

Singapore, from where I serve clients globally, also has meritocracy as a principle of governance. For instance, the education system is based on equality. Everyone is allowed the opportunity to succeed based on the same path that ends in the same tests, regardless of background. Education fees are relatively low, and grants are offered for low-income families. Depending on your mother tongue, you can select the language of focus in addition to English.

Yet, income inequality in both countries is high. I know of plenty of people around the world who do not have the same opportunities that I have benefitted from. And with a son who has attention deficit hyperactivity disorder—inherited from me, although I have a mild version—I know that schools cater to children who fit the mainstream. Is this meritocracy? It depends on how you define the merits—working hard using your abilities? How do we define abilities? If everyone has the same abilities— the ones that the school system is based on—we will be lacking in diversity and miss out on so much talent and fail to value people for their unique talents.

Nepotism

Nepotism is another deterrent to a true meritocracy. According to one study, 43 per cent of white admissions to Harvard University are recruited athletes, family members of alumni, people who donated to the university, and children of faculty and staff. *The Economist* reports that a white student who is near the bottom of the pack academically but has legacy status—such as a family member of alumni—has roughly the same chance of getting accepted as a typical Asian applicant in the top tenth percentile of applicants. In Princeton University's class of 2015, 33 per cent of those offered a spot were from the family of an alumni member.

In the Philippines, various sources tell me that it is well known that by paying bribes, you're allowed into the best schools. In 2019, numerous wealthy parents in the US were prosecuted for this practice. In a society where meritocracy is mythology, wealth and who we know are as important as what we know and how capable we are without those privileges.

Consider this: while the top inheritance or estate tax rate is 40 per cent, the average tax rate paid when your parents pass on is just 17 per cent, which is only paid on assets greater than US$5.3 million. You stand a better chance of becoming a millionaire by having the right parents than creating the next IT unicorn.

Let's be honest with ourselves. Since its independence in 1776, the US has been ruled by the elite and has primarily been a land of opportunity for the white, well-connected, able-bodied, straight, wealthy man at best. And in corporations, while nepotism is equally alive and well, the narrative of meritocracy persists as much as in other aspects of American society. And it is not helping those who have traditionally been under-represented.

Flaws of meritocracy

Scientist Dr Emma Smith* provides a demonstration of the flaws of meritocracy, which we so strongly believe exists. She shares an experience that dates back to 2019.

After being recruited for a leadership position, Dr Smith learned that a male colleague received more support than she received. 'We had a comparable project load, but he got a consultant to help. He could be relaxed in his job, while I had to work very hard.' In fact, she said, 'I constantly had to work harder than men to be where I am today.'

It isn't uncommon for women to be the 'good girls' and do what they are told, while men are more likely to *ask* for what they need and want, which gives them a better chance of *receiving* it.

In Dr Smith's case, it seems she was the victim of either outright discrimination or perhaps a subtler form of unconscious bias. Her male boss may have assumed that her male colleague was ambitious and wanted to achieve more, so that it was considered appropriate to hire an extra resource to work for him. The boss may not have thought about it at all, or he may have been used to the female scientists working hard and not complaining. He may have wanted to save on the limited resource budget and hired the extra resource for Dr Smith's male colleague.

Whatever the thought process behind the boss's decision, it resulted in systemic discrimination and bears no trace of meritocracy.

She also referred to the challenge of women and emotions on the job that we have discussed in the first myth. 'My direct boss labelled me "emotional" and didn't appreciate my passion,' according to Dr Smith. But luckily, one of her bosses recognized her passion for her job as a strength: 'The global R&D boss loved it.'

Dr Smith agrees that our systems have failed and points out that 'the best person for the job' is a comfortable argument to maintain the status quo. 'People who say this don't fully understand what it means. There is a true business case for diversity. Women do bring in other perspectives.'

Her story shows that companies often maintain unfair practices that present women with more obstacles to being promoted. Only 30 per cent of European women surveyed by McKinsey said their companies' evaluation system was gender neutral.[34] Typically, women work harder than men to get to a similar leadership level.[35]

'As a man,' Farberger, a trans woman, mentioned in a podcast, 'I genuinely thought, I falsely thought, that the playing field . . . was equal for everyone. But now in hindsight, I see all the privileges I had . . . as a white, heterosexual man.' She confirmed through her unique personal experience that there is no meritocracy in corporate life.

'Unfortunately, I needed a gender transition to actually see these privileges,' she states. I hope that more men will listen to Farberger and take women's real, lived experiences seriously and make corporate life more inclusive.

Incompetency in leadership

Dr Tomas Chamorro-Premuzic, professor of business psychology at University College London and Columbia University, and chief innovation officer at ManpowerGroup, also challenges the meritocracy myth in his work, which relies on international, cross-industry data. He argues that we promote too many incompetent men and that we can't distinguish between confidence and competence: 'Because [people in general] commonly misinterpret displays of confidence as a sign of competence, we are fooled into believing that men are better leaders than women.'[36, 37]

In his book, *Why Do So Many Incompetent Men Become Leaders?*, he wrote that the advantage that men have over women is that 'hubris'—excessive pride or self-assurance—is too often mistaken for executive ability, when the opposite is, in fact, true. He noted that 'pretty much anywhere in the world men tend to think that they are much smarter than women . . .'

We needed a man to state this in a best-selling book.

When I met him face-to-face in Singapore, he again stressed that arrogance and overconfidence are *inversely* related to leadership talent—the ability to build and maintain high-performing teams, and to inspire followers to set aside their selfish agendas and to work for the common interest of the group.

I asked him for his opinion on whether confidence is irrelevant for leadership. It's a point that I have been challenged on repeatedly when I quote him. 'Too much confidence in yourself leads to dishonesty about what is going on. We don't need leaders who can't say "I don't know."' He does allow us the kind of confidence that leads us to say 'I don't know'—in other words, a strong self-awareness of our competencies and limitations is healthy.

He described how we should focus much more on self-knowledge rather than self-belief. 'If you BS yourself, you will find it easier to BS others,' he added, referring to inflated egos and overconfidence that can lead to bad leadership.

Unlike confident men, women typically underestimate their skills and rarely boast about their achievements. For instance, in the US, women on average include 11 per cent fewer skills on their LinkedIn profile than men in similar jobs with similar levels of experience.[38] One study found that women sell themselves 33 per cent short of men.[39] The two (male) authors of the article conclude 'what's holding [women] back is not lack of capability but a dearth of opportunity. When given those opportunities, women are just as likely to succeed in higher-level positions as men.'[40]

Chamorro-Premuzic's book is provocative enough that when I present it in workshops, it's met with scepticism from women and men alike. Still, when asked how many companies have fallen prey to obvious mismanagement by highly paid executives, the participants hardly hold back in their criticism of failed leaders. And when I ask how many have worked for a boss less competent than themselves, almost everyone raises their hand. You can practically see the bad memories bubble up in every single person in the room.

I'm happy that a man stated this, and my purpose here is not to man-bash. There are loads of fantastic male leaders out there, and individuals with the same gender vary as much as—or substantially more than!—the statistical gender differences that studies show do exist. But as you'll see from the research in this chapter, there are also loads of highly competent female leaders who never get their well-deserved chance to lead, simply due to human bias and systemic failure.

Why do we continuously believe in the myth of meritocracy while most of us have seen plenty of people promoted about whom we ask ourselves 'How on earth did they get that job?'

Women as hyper-performers

There is plenty of evidence that the performance of girls and women is more than just on par with boys and men. Throughout the education system, girls and women achieve better grades than boys and men, by as much as 6.3 per cent.[41] Even in STEM (science, technology, engineering, and mathematics) subjects, girls score better. In Germany, men and women enter college in roughly equal numbers, but more women than men complete their degrees.[42] In Iceland, women at university outnumber men by two to one.[43] The proportion of tertiary-educated women is now higher than the proportion of tertiary-educated men in almost all OECD (Organisation for Economic Co-operation and Development) countries.[44]

Clearly, women are more than—and we could stress 'more than' if academic performance is a good yardstick—competent to contribute to the workforce on an equal footing with men.

Evidence also indicates that women have better leadership skills than men, which again strongly suggests that companies are not promoting true meritocracy. Jack Zenger and Joseph Folkman write in the *Harvard Business Review* that women outperform men in seventeen out of nineteen leadership skills.[45] Isn't this another indicator that we don't promote people into leadership positions based on a neutral evaluation of skills? Otherwise, many more women would be leaders. Especially considering women outperform men—on average—academically, as well as having a great foundation for the 'soft' skills needed in leadership.

I was quite surprised when presenting these facts in a workshop for the first time. A male participant felt that we were man-bashing. When I looked at the slides in my presentation afterwards, the slide was preceded and followed by a very neutral questions such as 'What great leaders come to mind?' The audience was urged to think about great leaders regardless of gender in the same context.

However, simply sharing the research that women outperform men on seventeen out of nineteen essential leadership skills is an uncomfortable truth that may feel like I was unjustly criticizing men.

This triggered me to tiptoe around the research and stress that 'I'm not saying that men are bad leaders' and 'There are good and bad leaders regardless of gender.' Meanwhile, in my talks, I tell men that if they feel wronged and criticized or if they feel that they are accused of being bad leaders then welcome to the club. That's what women have been told and what many women have consequently felt throughout civilization up until today. Isn't it about time that we correct this? It's had painful consequences for women for too long. We've been told that we are not natural leaders up until this research was published—and are often still being told today.

I'm merely presenting research, which puts women slightly above men. If some men feel that is man-bashing, it's because it is painful to realize that what they thought was an inborn privilege has just been taken away. Is it painful to have privileges taken away? Of course. A loss can be painful.

Back to the research. A quick Google or library search will show you that there is no consensus on how much time a leader should spend 'leading' versus completing tasks. Of course, this is probably largely dependent on the industry, function, and hierarchy level. Nevertheless, I'm sure we agree that inspiring and engaging a team, driving for results, developing others, collaboration and teamwork, and building relationships are better uses of a leader's time than writing reports or fixing equipment.

As it happens, the former points are just some of the skills where women outperform men.

The research, based on thousands of 360-degree reviews, has found that women score 5–7 percentage points higher on:

- Taking initiative
- Resilience
- Practising self-development
- Driving for results
- Displaying high integrity and honesty

More surprising to me was the fact that women equally outperform men on bold leadership, championing change, and establishing stretch goals.

By a much smaller margin than the previously mentioned skills, men outperform women on technical or professional expertise (1 percentage point) and developing a strategic perspective (1.3 percentage points).

The research confirms what I hear from the hundreds of female participants in MetaMind's Women in Leadership programmes. Many women are efficient at the workplace to go home as early as possible, where a second job awaits. When given extra responsibility, they take it on without loudly questioning it. They may resort to being 'nice' and want their work to speak for themselves, and when passed over for a promotion, they continue to keep a low profile while still tending their jobs. From the company point of view, you can't get better employees than this stereotype.

Let's shatter the narrative of meritocracy and the belief that 'we take the best person for the job' and promote more of the many highly capable women out there.

Equality versus equity

At the beginning of the school year, a first-grade teacher takes a bunch of plasters with colourful cartoons on them. 'We are going to do a pretend game,' she tells her young pupils. 'Imagine it hurts somewhere. I've got these nice plasters to put on it,' she says, while showing what are probably the coolest plasters for six-year-olds.

She gets one child to the front of the classroom and asks where their pain is. 'Here,' says the first child, holding up their index finger to show a pretend cut on the tip it. The teacher puts the plaster there. When the first child has been taken well care of, she starts walking around the classroom, and no matter where the other children say they have pain, they get a plaster on the same spot on the same finger as the first child.[46]

It isn't hard to imagine the children protesting 'That's not fair!' and 'But I hurt my knee!'—or arm, or nose while pointing to the diverse areas that they had pretended hurt.

The teacher demonstrated that we all have different needs. Putting a plaster on a spot that is perfectly healthy doesn't do any good. Neither does it help alleviate the pain.

Equality means giving everyone the same thing i.e., in this case, the plaster on their index finger regardless of where they had pain. Equity, on the other hand, means giving people what they truly need—putting the plaster where it hurts. So, the only way to be fair is to focus on equity, to respond to each person's *individual* needs.

Corporations, unfortunately, tend to be based on equality. We give everyone the same training programmes and an opportunity to apply for the same jobs. Most companies ask everyone to work the same or at least similar hours.

However, if a highly qualified person lacks confidence, why not provide an individual coaching programme to build confidence? If a potential leader doesn't have the industry connections required for a job, why not assign a mentor who can open doors or send them to the right industry conferences and meetings? If a parent needs to attend school meetings in the late afternoon, why not allow them the flexibility to go? If women lack the confidence that they can be leaders, why not create a safe space for women to find their way in a male-dominated world by sending them to Women in Leadership programmes? As we have seen, this is merely correcting past mistakes—we have told women they are not natural leaders, and the role models we have provided were often not making women see themselves as leaders.

We're focussing so much on equality that fairness is compromised.

There is an excellent business case for diversity and inclusion

There is a good argument for 'group meritocracy'. Instead of considering 'the best person for the job', organizations can gain from considering the best person for the team and for the company.

Research shows that companies in the top quartile for leadership diversity earn an additional 9 percentage points EBIT (earnings before interest and taxes).[47] That's a strong business case for hiring or promoting a woman, since the diversity she may provide in a male-dominated team is in itself likely to be better for the bottom line. Isn't it otherwise unheard of for a company to ignore an ethical and legal opportunity to earn an additional 9 percentage points of EBIT? Any CEO who ignores such a business opportunity would be promptly fired by shareholders and owners. But that is what is happening with inclusion—a business case is ignored or simply not given the investment needed to provide the full return. Hiring and promoting diversity is good for the company, so let's broaden our myopic view of who is the best for a job to who is the best for a company.

Too many women, as in Dr Smith's case, vote with their feet. Dr Smith resigned after an unsuccessful confrontation with her boss. Women resign because unfairness, rather than meritocracy, prevails. It was clear from my discussions with her that she's a highly competent, critical-thinking, eloquent, emotionally intelligent, and passionate scientist and leader. By failing to recognize her executive leadership potential, the company reduced their statistical chances of increasing their EBIT.

The obvious solution is to scrutinize companies for structural biases, to eliminate those biases, and to start promoting based on competence rather than confidence. It's time to face that meritocracy is a myth so that corporations can be braver in promoting women and other under-represented groups. Clearly, it's time to look at how we can give under-represented groups what they need to succeed because there is no question that individuals, companies, and society all stand to benefit from this. Diversity increases group intelligence,[48] because we are able to include more diverse perspectives and take better decisions.

Has your company reviewed their recruiting, appraisal, promotion, and reward processes to include the skills that women bring to the workplace? Have you looked at the possibility that, when interviewing candidates, you may be fooled by self-confidence, overlooking candidates who are immensely talented yet humble? Are you giving enough opportunities to the many competent women in your company to prove their leadership capabilities?

These are important questions for today's leaders to ask in order to create more diverse, and thus more successful, companies.

Countering the myth that we have a meritocracy

If you're in a position to argue for group meritocracy, equity over equality, promoting women based on fairness, and a gender-neutral competence set, here are some potential statements you can use:

- 'Since women typically keep a lower profile about their achievements, plus typically underestimate their own skills, how about you take a chance on promoting a few women that are very likely just humble? They may turn out to have much more depth than you think.'
- 'Confidence and boasting are not good indicators of performance, yet our systems are still biased towards hiring overconfident people. It's natural to be fooled by this, but we aren't doing our jobs well unless we use the right predictive indicators for job success when hiring and promoting.'
- 'Women's skills and motivation to have a career are regularly dismissed. They are dismissed as leadership potential, are asked to do menial tasks such as fetching coffee and taking minutes. They have to work harder to prove themselves, get fewer stretch assignments and fewer opportunities to meet more senior leaders. Doesn't this mean that when a woman has gotten as far as her male peer, she's proven to be at least as qualified, and maybe even more qualified than her male peer?'

- 'Women outperform men on seventeen out of nineteen leadership skills. How about we review the recruiting, appraisal, development, promotion, and reward processes by looking at these skills and ensure our processes are not biased?'
- 'As a man, you can do a lot for gender balance if you embrace some of the leadership styles that are considered feminine. By embracing compassion, humility, and empathy as leadership principles, you can pave the way for leadership to be associated with any gender and truly based on meritocracy.'
- 'In schools, women score higher than men. In wealthier countries, women are attending university more often than men. Where do we get the notion that women are not competent? If we don't have women in leadership, where are we going wrong? Where is our company going wrong?'
- 'Academic tests are less ambiguous than appraisals in the workplace. In exam papers, any indication of gender can be eliminated. So, isn't it highly unlikely that women, who statistically get better grades at school, should have lower performance in the workplace? Isn't it much more likely that our evaluation of female candidates is biased?'
- 'What do we need to do differently to eliminate all evaluation bias and give equal opportunity to all?'

Myth Three

'Women Can't Work Together'

Gossip, microaggressions, cliques, and exclusion—*that's what you get when women work together, right?*

How many times have I heard this claim? Every time a women-led project goes just slightly wrong, we use it to confirm the narrative that 'Women can't work together.'

I'm the founder and chair of a non-profit initiative called KeyNote Women Speakers—KeyNote Women in short. The initiative is on a mission to bring more diversity to global speaking stages. Dozens of female volunteers have rallied around this vision that the world's speaking stages will one day represent the diversity of its people, including gender balance.

One project within the initiative went wrong. Agreements were twisted, the volunteer who had put her hand up to lead the project was excluded, instructions from the leader were ignored, and information was withheld.

The project was completed, but with unnecessary friction. After the main part had been completed, nobody on the team had the energy to make the project flourish. Even volunteers who had committed to follow up felt the negative energy and pulled out. A project that could have been core to the organization and led to many follow-up projects simply fizzled out.

Is this yet another story to prove that women aren't capable of working together?

No!

If women couldn't work together, we wouldn't have been able to build a world-leading directory of women speakers with the sole help of dozens of female volunteers within the first three years. A single project—just one of many—in the first five years suffered from a lack of collaboration.

Consider how often we experience discord, exclusion, ignored opinions, withheld information, twisted agreements, and people who further their own agendas in mixed or male-dominated projects. In my experience, this is true in most organizations on a daily basis. So why don't we say that men can't work together? Why do we single out women whenever one of their projects goes awry?

Sheryl Sandberg, former chief operating officer of Meta and co-founder of the Lean In Foundation, said, 'Women aren't any meaner to women than men are to one another. Women are just expected to be nicer. We stereotype men as aggressive, and women as kind. When women violate these stereotypes, we judge them harshly.'[49] In other words, we hold women to higher standards.

Sandberg's quote shows that the double bind is at play again.

One stereotype is that women engage in more mean gossip than men. But research shows that while women may be more likely to share *neutral* information about others when the subject of the conversation is absent, they *don't* engage in more *negative* gossip than men.[50]

While conducting research for their book, *It's Not You, It's the Workplace*, authors Alton B. Harris and Andrea S. Kramer noted in a *Harvard Business Review* article that there was 'no empirical evidence supporting the notion that women are more mean-spirited, antagonistic, or untrustworthy in dealing with other women than men are in dealing with other men.'[51]

The fact is, we come across egos everywhere, regardless of gender. It is difficult to work with people. If my experience at KeyNote Women is anything to go by, I'm quite happy that the project that went horribly wrong proved to be the exception, not the rule.

And there are plenty of women who work well together. Take Natasha Williams, a leader in the tech industry: 'I have a female boss at the moment, so life is like a dream,' she shared. 'In fact, my immediate boss, as well as my most senior boss, are both female. Compared to having male bosses, the difference is the lack of microaggressions. I'm being treated like a human,' she explained. She expressed that with her last male boss, she was made to feel incompetent purely because she was a woman. And she couldn't get it right with him. 'I felt underutilized, so I looked for and took on other projects, since I was being underutilized and wanted to prove I was more than competent, he said I was too confident. I could never succeed or even just exist as I am because I was seen by him with all the biases he had built up over the years against women.' She continued with her explanation of why it was a 'dream' working with female bosses: 'With my current boss I have my job—I either do it, do it badly or do it with areas of improvement. There is no assumption of ineptitude or specific consideration because of my gender.'

So regardless of their reputation, women aren't meaner, nor are they cold, aggressive, unsupportive, or manipulative b******. Women are simply held to higher standards than men.

Queen Bee syndrome

The Queen Bee syndrome was coined about half a century ago[52] and refers to women in leadership positions who treat other women on their team worse than men, purely because of gender. Madeleine Albright, late former US Secretary of State, famously said that there is 'a special place in hell' for women who don't support other women i.e., Queen Bees.

A Queen Bee may feel that there is space for only one woman. This may be justified, or it may merely be her perception, especially if she's the 'token' or 'quota' woman in her department or organization. Queen Bee behaviour may then be a woman's defence for keeping her single spot at the top. Tokenism and very low quotas for having women in leadership may have been programming women to see other women as competition.

I encountered a Queen Bee at my first corporate job in the 1990s. As a fresh MBA graduate, I was supposed to be motivated by speaking to a female role model. This proposed role model was the most senior woman in the company, at a C-level minus two. I simply thought that not having women on A- and B-levels in the company in the nineties was a scandal in its own right. I was hoping that I would be among the women who could have a career that changed the make-up of the company. I was pretty ignorant, but that's a different story.

Not only was I totally *demotivated* by her behaviour, but I felt sorry for her. In our discussions, there was no trace of support or desire to support me. Instead, she was cold and distant, speaking with an air of scientific arrogance. She offered her one piece of advice: 'If you want a career, forget about having a family,' implying that unrelenting hard work was the only way to get to her level, and that having a career and children were incompatible—for women. She didn't show any signs of believing in gender equality.

Research by the Center for Creative Leadership has an explanation as to why the system promotes Queen Bees. Apparently, there is a penalty for women who promote women, both in terms of competency and performance ratings.[53] It seems that unless you're the CEO, you'll get punished for promoting people from your own underprivileged group. Men, however, are not penalized for this.

As a side remark, this makes it difficult for women when humans have 'affinity bias,' which means that we gravitate towards people like us. One outcome is that we are more likely to promote people like ourselves—our gender, our skin colour, and our education.

The harsh truth is that women have faced a penalty for promoting other women, while men typically promote men—and have done so throughout history, obviously without negative consequences.

Generally, Queen Bees have broken the glass ceiling, so they may feel better believing that they've attained their position due to their talent and hard work. Believing they *deserve* it feels better than accrediting success to a mentor who supported them or a lucky coincidence of being in the right place at the right time. Or they might see their struggles to become a leader as 'normal' and even necessary.

'I think more of the nastiness happens in the more senior roles as the pyramid gets narrower. Already, women have so few seats at important tables. And then, instead of being allies, for some reason, they oppose each other. They are more threatened by each other rather than supporting each other,' Pravin[*] told me. 'This woman was doing everything that she could to really push me off the plank,' Pravin shared about a former colleague. She felt very victimized by what sounded like a female bully in a former job. She was able to cope with it for a while thanks to another female leader at the time, who recognized the toxicity that was going on.

A hypothesis is that quotas—especially when the quotas are low—mean that a small number of women get the very limited executive positions. This may place women in direct competition with one another for fewer available leadership opportunities and create Queen Bees.

To quota or not

I hear a lot of complaints about quotas, including one from a friend's husband. 'It's just gone too far,' he says over dinner at their place. 'I have been asked to hire a woman from one of the ASEAN countries who is in her twenties and gay. And my industry is very male dominated. It's an impossible task,' he lamented.

I find it difficult to take the comment at face value. It's hard to believe that there is such a strict requirement on the profile of a candidate. I could imagine that this was a suggested list of criteria and not to be seen as the full list where all boxes have to be checked. It would be difficult to find a single person in the entire country who would have the right profile, let alone with the desired qualifications. Needless to say, if this were a true story, their implementation of quotas is doomed to fail.

I am strongly of the opinion that we need quotas. For the past few decades, we have been focussing on gender equality. Companies have had an abundance of time to change things. Since that hasn't worked, we need to try different approaches. We can make it work with some mindset shifts. For instance, a gender quota is not a punishment for men. It is a tool to compensate for the additional obstacles that women face in advancing their careers, whether in business, academia, or politics.

In my work with companies across virtually all industries, I also see a tremendous shift when you shift the narrative from: 'This is not possible' to 'How can we make this possible?' An approach where we open the mind to possibility is leading to much better outcomes.

Norway was in such a situation. In 2003, Norway became the first country to introduce a whopping quota of 40 per cent women on the boards of listed companies.[54] There was no impact on profitability or bottom line, despite fears from the business community that this would be the case. And for proponents of diversity, it is also interesting to note that the usual benefits of diversity did not set in.

Norway gave companies two years to comply and threatened dissolution if targets were unmet. This may be the reason for the quick change—non-compliance had severe consequences.

Most countries and companies have quotas that are around the 30 per cent-mark. This has good reasons. We know that diversity increases group intelligence[55, 56] —if there is a minimum number of diverse people. Diversity is not likely to lead to differences in results if it doesn't lead to inclusion. And with a more diverse group around, it is more likely for people to listen to and accept different views. One study puts the advantage of diversified teams at a threshold of 20 per cent that must be surpassed.[57] Others show the benefits when we are closer to 30 per cent,[58] which is the reason why many companies, especially those in traditionally male industries, have 30 per cent as their gender diversity target. Companies such as Unilever and Barilla, who hire from streams that are not as traditionally male dominated like, for instance, STEM, are often much more ambitious in their 50/50 gender targets.

Needless to say, there are other components that are essential for diversity to have an impact on the bottom line. Corporate culture must be managed to ensure that everyone feels safe to speak up and share ideas; without a culture of innovation, you will not have innovation.

Are Queen Bees real?

I have found research about Queen Bees inconclusive. Credit Suisse's gender report[59] dismisses the concept of Queen

Bees altogether, suggesting that it's more fiction than fact that a successful woman 'pulls the ladder up and makes it difficult for women to succeed her'. The study provides data that successful women are much more likely to surround themselves with other women, appointing them to senior positions more frequently than their male counterparts.

Their research shows that it isn't necessarily the women who don't support other women, but the men who don't support women. In one study of 1,500 S&P companies, there was strong evidence of an implicit quota. When one woman reached senior management, it was 51 per cent less likely that a second woman would make it—blocked not by a Queen Bee, but by a male CEO. When the CEO was female, the opposite was more likely to be true. It was more likely that a second woman would get promoted.

I don't believe there is a clear line to say whether Queen Bees are real or whether women support other women. It depends on the place and time. Sometimes, women may face a penalty for supporting other women. A C-suite level woman from a multi-billion Euro company once told me that she had to be very careful not to be seen getting too involved in gender-equality topics, because her male C-suite peers would not take her seriously if she did. The media already positioned her as a woman rather than a competent businessperson, and her being a darling of the business media was somewhat of a red rag to a bull, in the testosterone-filled boardroom.

It's back to: Women are not unable to collaborate. Society has created an unhealthy basis for women to support each other.

Why women may get into each other's hair

You may see a tendency for women to fight for a top job when there is a culture of tokenism. Tokenism is about hiring people with a different profile for display and paying lip-service to diversity and inclusion practices. You can describe it as diversity without inclusion. When there is a feeling of scarcity and competition, people start competing against each other, as history has proven many times. If there is only space for one person, or very few, there will naturally be more competition for that position among under-represented demographic groups.

'In my previous company's leadership team, there were two women. The moment you would put these women together in a room, they would start fighting. The men would look at each other with an expression that said, "What just happened there?" We started having meetings outside the meeting, which led to many other problems,' Sean O'Connor* shared his experience with senior women in-fighting. When I challenged him that this may be because the quota system means that some women may feel that there is only space for one woman at the top, he responded, 'I don't think this explains everything. At my current company, there are a handful of women in relatively senior roles. Women are supported. Our global CEO is a woman. Our new Asia CEO is a woman. Our CEO has a strong pro-female agenda. We're better than most regarding promoting women.'

When we support the promotion of token women, or token minority representatives in general, they are much more likely to adapt to the culture of the power group. They may overplay the behaviour that made them successful in the past, rather than focus on the values inherent in their diversity, forfeiting the purpose of diversity.

However, at O'Connor's company, there is a good proportion of woman in executive positions.

'The women leaders in my organization can be rude. This is not a feature of the company. We are polite,' O'Connor added. 'I don't get it. Don't they realize that they were picked because of who they are, rather than who someone else is?'

'We even have a women's network where men are encouraged to participate. Why don't women stick together? If you put a few Irish people in the office, they would immediately form a clique.' O'Connor was asking himself more than me, it seemed.

When I turned the question back to O'Connor, he reflected: 'We all have our "derailers"; the ways that we behave out of character when we are under stress. Perhaps women feel that they need to work doubly hard to prove themselves. I don't know. Perhaps we are too afraid of giving them negative feedback and simply accept their aggressive behaviour.'

I have not carried out a workplace assessment of this company—this is just one interview. But it is an important observation from a person who works for a company that takes gender balance seriously and who defines himself as a male ally.

It's an important reminder that many different factors are at play. Sometimes it is just people not getting along. We all have our darker sides. I personally am very collaborative and am mostly competitive with myself until I'm triggered. I'm very much a giver, but if you start being too loud about something that I see as my turf and choose to ignore me—I get competitive.

Times are changing

The good news is that many agree that the Queen Bee syndrome, if it truly exists, is a generational issue. Women are showing that they are great collaborators. More women are assuming leadership roles as they slowly find more female role models around them. Nevertheless, Fortune 500 companies had a meagre 8.8 per cent of female CEOs in 2022, so there is still a long way to go before we reach gender parity.

On the good news front, leadership styles are also changing to include more of what we typically describe as 'feminine' traits. This means that women don't have to behave like men to succeed, which frequently happened in the past and led top women to reject their softer sides and become harsh. Think of perhaps the most famous female leader in the 1980s—Margaret Thatcher, the Iron Lady.

Luckily, today, we're more likely to accept the softer side of leadership that puts humans first, whether it's Salesforce's Marc Benioff or New Zealand's former Prime Minister Jacinda Ardern, leaders known for their empathetic, supportive, and human-focussed leadership styles. And as the context for women who managed to climb the career ladder changes, there is less need for them to behave 'more male than the men'.

Reframing 'feminine' and 'masculine' leadership styles would, in my view, help us lead with our strong leadership traits regardless of our gender. We can reframe 'feminine' traits as collaborative traits: nurturing, empowering, caring, empathy, team play. 'Male' traits can be reframed as competitive traits: assertiveness, being a go-getter. I am convinced that when men increasingly embrace leading with empathy and nurturing their teams, the road is paved for anyone, regardless of gender, to become a leader.

Having worked with many women, including leading and facilitating a network of senior female leaders, my personal experience is that most women today are very supportive of other women. A comparable mixed network group that I facilitate (mixed unfortunately means that it is at least 90 per cent male) is by far not as mutually supportive as the women's network. In my personal experience, Queen Bees are a phenomenon of days gone by.

A tendency that I have observed is that women introduce themselves in a more personal way then men do. They may start with 'I'm passionate about . . .' or 'What I love about my job is . . .' or 'It's challenging to . . .' When I have a mixed group of people in my networking meetings, I make sure to invite a woman to introduce herself first. It often sets the tone for the rest of the group, including the men, to not resort to a bragging introduction like, 'I am the MD for company so-and-so, a multi-billion-dollar business.'

I find this sets a tone for openness to meet each other at a different level and collaboration. It certainly is not compatible with the narrative that women don't collaborate.

The bottom line is that women don't have a gene that hinders them from collaborating, nor do they engage in more mean-spirited gossip than men do. They aren't meaner; they just have more obstacles to cross and are expected to be nicer in the attempt. And it can be very challenging to deal with people— regardless of gender.

Combatting the myth that women can't work together

How do you respond when someone claims that women can't work together? Here are a few suggestions.

- 'The truth is: it can be very challenging to work with people.'
- 'In my experience, women work well together, especially when we're in a psychologically safe space.'
- 'There's a double bind at play. If a woman is a bad leader or bad collaborator, we assume it's because she's a woman. When a man is a bad leader or bad collaborator, we assume he just has leadership or collaboration deficits.'
- 'If there is rivalry in the workplace between women, it has nothing to do with their gender and everything to do with the stereotypes and biases they confront at work. For instance, if they aren't seen as caring and collaborative, they're labelled as "cold" and "mean". On top of that, if the organization gives the impression that there's only

space for a few women leaders, it's natural that women start competing. How can we work together to eliminate these root causes?'

- 'I haven't met a Queen Bee for a long time. I have a female boss/superior who or a female network that supports me and is very collaborative.'

- 'In previous generations, this myth was perhaps more pronounced than today. I certainly don't experience it now.'

- 'If she was a man, how would you describe the situation? Would you see it as having anything to do with gender?'

- 'Women are often held to higher standards than men and penalized if they're assertive. But then, when they aren't assertive, they're largely ignored.'

- 'Since assertiveness in women is seen negatively, unlike the way it's seen in men, it's possible that the Queen Bee term is used against women who are simply trying to do their jobs.'

- 'Since women are at risk of being penalized for promoting under-represented groups, leaving fewer jobs for women, it's only natural for competitiveness and defence mechanisms to set in among women. The solution is very simple: Include more diverse executives . . . *fast.*'

- 'We can avoid this by making companies truly inclusive in terms of opportunities for growth and development.'

- 'The solution is to have open discussions on desired leadership styles and to address behaviour that's out of line. We must correct this problem by providing systems and cultures that support inclusion, as well as offer coaching to help leaders develop the desired behaviours.'

- 'In companies that nurture an environment where women are scrutinized and feel that there is only space for one woman at the top, women may feel unnecessarily threatened and act accordingly.'

Myth Four

'We Don't Have a Gender Pay Gap Here'

'There is no pay gap when you adjust it to factors such as experience. It's all misleading headlines.' These are the words I was told by a male leader who considers himself an ally.

I certainly agree that headlines are misleading, but not in the same way this leader believes. According to the Global Gender Gap Report 2022 by World Economic Forum,[60] not only is the gender pay gap real but it will also take until 2154 for gender pay parity to be achieved based on current projections. Sadly, the trend was towards a growing chasm during the COVID-19 pandemic.

Although outright discrimination is illegal in most countries, the lack of pay transparency makes it difficult for anyone to claim equal pay. Transparent salary reporting and mandatory equal pay, as enforced in Iceland, would be helpful.[61] But with different measures of 'fairness' and biases prevailing, it becomes easy to believe that it will take 132 years to close the global gender gap.[62]

For example, in Australia, women earn on average 13.4 per cent less than men.[63] In Singapore, the pay gap between men and women for equal work stands at 6 per cent.[64]

Notice the wording of each of these statistics. Their differences can make the data confusing. There are two main concepts. One is to measure the difference in income between men and women. That's what Australia's 13.4 per cent is. The other is to measure what women versus men earn when they are in similar jobs, which is the equal pay for equal work concept. That's the figure of 6 per cent from Singapore.

Most companies measure the latter and claim that there is either no gender pay gap or an insignificant one at best. People who make this claim fail to recognize that functions in companies such as HR and communications are paid less than the business function. HR and communications are also functions that are typically female dominated, which means that we systematically devalue jobs typically held by women.

The leader who argued that headlines about the gender gap are deceptive held a common opinion of fairness when two people on the same level—say, product managers A and B—earn the same. He also mentioned, 'Supporting functions simply don't add the same value as marketing or sales does because it's further away from the core business.' I've heard this argument many times. Communications is a function dominated by women, so society tends to downplay its importance and regards jobs typically held by men as more valuable. Thus, the gap in earnings is created.

The World Economic Forum report revealed that the greatest challenge preventing the economic gender gap from closing is women's under-representation in emerging and well-paid roles. In cloud computing, just 12 per cent of professionals are women as reported by the World Economic Forum's 'Global Gender Gap Report 2020'.[65] In 2022, the percentage of women working in the well-paying AI sector stood at 30 per cent, which is a slow 4 percentage point increase since 2016.[66]

Research in Denmark also shows that between 1969 and 2019, professions that shifted towards female representation had a negative pay development. For instance, throughout this fifty-year period, as more women went into teaching in primary and secondary education, the profession saw a decline in income.

The same trend is currently happening in the medical field as more women are opting for the profession. At the same time, jobs that were typically held by men have moved up the pay scale.[67]

Even when jobs are the same, there can be vast discrepancies. In 2018, news reports emerged that actress Michelle Williams was paid US$1,000 for reshooting work as the female lead in the movie *All the Money in the World*. In comparison, her co-star Mark Wahlberg pocketed almost 'all the money,' or US$1.5 million, for the same reshooting work as the male lead. That's 1,500 times or 150,000 per cent more than the female lead's pay.[68] The fact that both actors were managed by the same talent agency and were in comparable roles didn't prevent their contracts from being startlingly different in terms of compensation. It was a chilling reminder that the systemic gender pay gap is deeply ingrained.

After the news about the film caused outrage around the world, the studio, the agency, and Wahlberg all pledged to donate certain portions of their revenue to charitable causes. Michelle Williams said that she merely felt numb about it. As an actress who grew up in the system, she was far from surprised, knowing full well that women in the entertainment industry are routinely treated unfairly.

Men are prioritized

It's true that women are more reluctant to negotiate salaries, so some leaders consciously or subconsciously assume women don't 'need' the money. 'I was once told I don't need as much salary because I am a woman,' Saniha Jafri, a female executive in Pakistan, told me. It may be assumed that we have well-earning husbands or even if we are single, we don't 'need' the money as much as our male peers, who are assumed to be 'family providers' and 'breadwinners'. And we say that our world is a meritocracy?!

Where's the fairness in women not being paid for the value they add?

The faculty member at Penn State whom I mentioned in the first chapter also said that when she was doing a post-doctoral degree, she had a great boss who was a very nice guy, 'but he was paying me peanuts. I heard from his assistant that he had said that I have a husband who will take care of me, and that was the reason for paying me very little. Because I was a woman and because I have a husband.' Asking women like her to negotiate is little use, because, as she said, 'I've never had much luck with asking for higher salary.'

I have personally experienced a 23 per cent pay gap. At that point in time, it was equal to that country's statistical gender pay gap.

When I was hired to work in Germany for the same company as my now husband, I had a slightly higher salary due to my MBA-accredited studies. Then, my husband was offered a job abroad, and we had decided to go together. You could argue that was the first mistake, and I only have myself to blame for focussing on 'us' rather than on 'me' because wanting a career requires a more egocentric attitude.

As part of the management trainee programme, my name was also mentioned in discussions for assignments abroad, but he was offered one in Japan before me.

I had already worked in China, graduated in Mandarin studies, and felt I was at least as qualified to work in Japan as my husband, who did not have a comparable Asian experience. At least I could read a little Japanese after having studied Chinese characters and had years of Asian experience. Getting an internal transfer for me was an uphill battle, even when there was a vacancy which matched my competencies. 'We don't want to set precedent for all wives to expect to get work when their husbands are coming to work here,' the conservative German boss in Japan said. 'Why don't you just spend the time having a couple of kids while you are there,' the much more modern HR leader in Germany advised me.

I did get a project assignment for six months. It was extended for two months. And two months. And so, it continued. I went to work several times without knowing whether my contract had been extended.

Fast forward almost a decade, and we had worked various places in Asia. Each time, I'd had to fight for my position, sometimes working for other companies, sometimes getting a contractual assignment. My husband and I were also working at a similar level despite my constant fight for my place in corporate life, him being served stretch assignments, and top leadership development programmes with extensive training and support along the way.

One day, it was time for us 'to go back home', as my husband's bosses said. We had to leave Japan to go work in Germany. 'It's better for the family,' they claimed to know despite my husband being offered a lateral move, me being in a job that provided a career outlook and that I truly enjoyed, our kids loving their Japanese kindergartens, and Germany in my wildest dreams not being 'home' to me. I was born in Denmark, grew up in the Netherlands, and had lived in Asia three times as long as in Germany. The kids had never been there and one of them barely spoke the language. There was nothing 'home' about Germany.

My Japanese boss at the time, a senior executive in the organization, was very supportive of me and saw me as a high potential candidate. Unfortunately, that did not convince anybody in headquarters. I was told 'We don't know you in Germany, you need to come back and start over,' because I had been given local project assignments along the way and had not been registered on the global high-flyer list in contrast to my husband. That I was on a seniority level similar to my husband and got top performance ratings did not carry any weight, neither did the lobbying by my Japanese boss.

A few years later again, I was offered a promotion from my 'starting over' position and up to a similar level on which my husband was. I had a 23 per cent pay gap compared to him—which our bank statement every month reminded me about.

When I got the promotion offer, I asked whether the pay gap of 23 per cent could be closed. 'Of course!' was the senior leader's response, 'How on earth did that happen?' When I was offered a 5 per cent increase a week or so later, I inquired what happened to the remainder of the 23 per cent. 'I'll look into it,' was his response. I was offered another 5 per cent, taking it to a 10 per cent increase in total. Again, I called my future boss to understand what happened to closing the pay gap. His secretary first was very friendly on the phone, saying he was in a meeting and would call me back later. He didn't. When I called half an hour later, her tone changed and she informed me that he was not available.

The promotion offer was withdrawn. The big boss in my division told me I had 'gone too far' after the two senior leaders had spoken.

The only explanation I can find is that the company could not deal with a woman pointing out an inequality, and when she wasn't taking peanuts by falling on her knees in appreciation and instead questioning their own previous commitments, they couldn't deal with the situation. Subconsciously, of course. In reality, they blamed the woman for misreading the situation by not accepting 10 per cent—when in fact, 23 per cent had been the topic of discussion.

While being accused of not being appreciative of getting 10 per cent, when a gap of 23 per cent was the issue on the table, I experienced:

- Men being given bigger pay raises than what they asked for.
- Male colleagues getting bonuses that positively surprised them.
- Colleagues saying, 'He needs a pay rise because he has a family to support.'
- HR stating, 'She doesn't need the money because her husband works.'

Luckily, such instances are not as commonplace as when this happened to me in 2006, but what we must remember is that a foregone pay increase from decades ago has a huge impact for our lifelong income potential. Losing out on $10,000 one year (which can easily be the case, considering a pay gap of 10–25 per cent is not unheard of) will become $300,000 of loss of income after 30 years—easy math. If we consider the compound interest of just $1,000 in a foregone increase one year 'because she has a husband and she doesn't need the pay,' we are looking at a loss of lifetime income of over $47,000 if that money is invested at a realistic interest rate, of 3 per cent or so. Meaning if a woman is hired for $1,000 less than her male counterpart, or in an early stage misses out on that same amount and gets all the increases that her male counterpart gets, she is missing out on what consists of a year's salary for many.

This is not even considering what a loss of income for absence during maternity leave or other care leave, or part-time work will amount to. You can imagine the amount we are looking at if the $1,000 that you miss out on at the beginning of your career can compound to so much if you invest it instead. Many women may today be missing out on fortunes due to the compound effect of lower increases years back.

This is again showing that we have no meritocracy at all—regardless of what proponents claim.

Some companies show the way that the pay gap can be closed. 'It's a big time investment and, in reality, it is very complicated. Age, seniority, performance, location, job grade are some of the factors that need to be included in the calculations,' explained Federico Vescovi, President of Barilla in Asia, Africa, Australia. He has put a lot of effort into ensuring that the unjustified pay gap is eliminated. The unjustified pay gap was closed in 2020. 'I will insist on us looking at it again yearly, because if you are not very vigilant, it may sneak in again.' Our biases cause unfairness to sneak in if we are not constantly on guard.

The 'mummy penalty'

The leader who believed there was no gender pay gap added an argument: 'If a woman decides to go on maternity leave, of course she's going to trail behind the man in terms of pay. It would be unfair to the man if she would earn as much as him.'

What measure of fairness is this? Biology has determined that women are the ones to carry babies. Companies and society say that the woman needs to go on maternity leave and often barely grant leave for dads. Women are providing future consumers and employees for the business world. As a 'thank you', women receive less pay, resulting in less state pension in old age. With a longer life expectancy, this means they must survive on less for longer than men even if they have had a comparable career. The penalty is long-term and unrelentingly punishing—remember the compound effect.

Companies, and society as a whole, simply value the tracks that men traditionally take more than those of women, and they pay men more because of it. The business world has been developed by men for men, and we see fairness with male eyes. Shouldn't we rethink our remuneration attitudes from a gender-neutral or gender-inclusive perspective?

For one thing, raising children is hardly the irrelevant experience it has been considered. Multitasking, effective communication, persuasion, mediation, negotiation, emotional intelligence, and leadership are all core business skills that are practised by any committed parent on a daily basis. Plus, taking a step back from what we do every day can provide us with a completely different perspective to our work. This can encourage out-of-the-box thinking and new ideas that can be applied in the workplace.

This was certainly my personal experience. I have been a communication expert and people manager during my corporate life. But it was when I had children that I was most challenged to practise those skills every day. I grew professionally, as well as personally, during my parental leave.

Even if equal pay laws are more effectively enforced, wider structural and socio-cultural problems may persist. Men were historically the primary earners, while women were in charge of caregiving. Based on a now outdated view of gender roles, motherhood and unpaid care work in general have had a profound and enduring effect on women's relationship with the labour market.[69] According to a UN Women report,[70] women dedicate on average 3.2 times more hours to unpaid care work than men. A 2021 study by the Center for Global Development found that, in 2020, women took on 173 more hours of unpaid childcare— the unpaid care for their own families—while men took on just 59 more hours.[71]

This 'invisible' work contributes at least US$10.8 trillion a year to the global economy[72] and encompasses both reproductive and productive work on which humanity and economies depend.

Yet, it remains heavily ignored. The burden of handling the bulk of unpaid labour plus the disadvantage of 'mummy penalty' takes a heavy toll on women's ability to have the same qualifications and speed of career development as their male counterparts. These are some common underlying structural and systemic reasons why women end up unable to compete with men in the labour force.

While I will discuss the mummy penalty in more depth in the next chapter, it makes sense here to reconsider how we perceive fairness. Not only do women receive less pay for equal work, but they also don't get paid at all for the house and care work to which they disproportionally contribute.

In sum, the gender pay gap is real, extensive, and subject to many assumptions and biases. Therefore, it needs urgent attention, not just for equity and fairness but also because it is typically women who suffer a significant loss of lifetime income and growth as a result.

How to counter the myth that the gender pay gap has been closed

If you are told that the gender pay gap has been closed, here are some of the responses you can give:

- 'We automatically devalue jobs when women become higher represented in that profession, industry, or line of business. Jobs that women choose are often worse paid and considered more non-essential. This ignores that many of these jobs are very essential—and many even critical, as we discovered nurses, typically women, to be during the COVID-19 pandemic.
- 'Occupations chosen by women are often under-valued. Often, these jobs focus on people and purpose rather than pure profits. Business is moving towards a realization that

people and purpose are as important as profit. Isn't it time that we start to reflect this in the pay these jobs receive?'

- 'Women are often less comfortable in negotiating than men. And women are often penalized when they are "leaning too far out of the window". In addition, women often have less self-confidence and ego than men because society teaches them to be more selfless and nurturing towards others. As a result, women may not ask for salary increases as much as men do. How can we make sure that all genders are given what they fairly deserve, rather than basing salaries on individual's self-confidence, negotiation skills and biases that men "need it because they are breadwinners"?'

- 'If you say that all genders are paid for equal work, have you considered that we're using male criteria to define "equal"? For instance, you risk ignoring the vast experience in multitasking, negotiation, stress resistance, resilience, communication, patience, dealing with different perspectives, and much more that parenthood and parental leave provide, and which women are still more likely to take than men. Essential leadership skills for the modern workplace are developed during parental leave.'

- 'Men are still more likely to work in better-paid firms and sectors, while women are more likely to work in sectors or firms where most staff are female and low paid, particularly if they work part-time. To address this, workforce strategies must ensure that women are better equipped (in terms of improved skills or reskilling) to take advantage of the opportunities of the Fourth Industrial Revolution. The questions we must ask are: How can we stop automatically devaluing the work that women typically carry out better? And what do we need for women to feel more confident in seeking employment in higher paying industries, functions, and jobs?'

Myth Five

'Mothers Aren't Committed to Work'

Natasha Williams is an engineer by training and holds a leadership role in the tech industry. She was working in her native Australia when she was pregnant with her daughter. 'The company had fabulous policies for maternity leave. However, my manager's mother hadn't worked, and his wife stopped working when they had children.' Her manager was used to women staying home after they had children.

'He told me over and over again, "You don't want to continue to work once you have children," "You'll not want this job back," "This is not going to be important to you." He had a replacement for me while I was on maternity leave and because he legally couldn't give my job away, he kept on calling me telling me I didn't want it.' On top of this, Williams shared, he argued that the person who was doing the job needed her job because they had a mortgage. 'I have a mortgage to pay, too!' she burst out to me, clearly exasperated.

'It's a woman who is pregnant thing,' she concluded. 'You're not taken seriously as soon as you are pregnant.'

I was told by my big—male—boss when I was pregnant with our firstborn that 'You don't know what you will feel when a child is there. I know that women don't want to work any more.' I tried to argue hard that I might know better than him what

I wanted, especially because I come from a culture where women do continue work as before after a maternity break. But both Williams and I experienced that it is difficult to argue against someone with strong conservative views. Neither of us were able to truly convince them what we knew would be best for us.

Parents and commitment to work

Even if you're against growing—or even maintaining—your country's birth rate, I'm sure you respect the biological urge to have sex, which has the side effect of reproduction, and build a family. It's written in our DNA.

Reproduction is a basic human function that most of us don't escape, yet it doesn't have a visible impact on men's working lives. Biologically, it's women who are not only the most physically affected by childbirth but also the most emotionally affected. The World Health Organization advises mothers worldwide to 'exclusively breastfeed infants for the child's first six months to achieve optimal growth, development and health',[73] typically resulting in emotional bonding. So yes, there is a period when mothers are most affected while they play their part in ensuring the health of their offspring.

There is also such a thing as 'baby brain', where the body produces hormones to ensure that the mother focuses on the well-being of the child. Post-delivery exhaustion is very common in the first few weeks after childbirth, and post-delivery fatigue may continue well into the second year after a child is born,[74] coinciding with the time that parents have more responsibilities on their plates.[75]

Does this mean that women aren't committed at work? In my experience, this is mostly an assumption projected on to women by society. It has turned into a narrative that hinders women from getting the opportunities they need to advance their careers.

A woman of childbearing age may not be hired at all, as the company might think, 'Oh, she's in her thirties, so she won't be reliable because she may go on maternity leave soon.' Or a woman may be passed over for stretched assignments and promotions, as companies may think, 'As a mother, she won't be able to put in the necessary effort.'

Mike Cook, the former CEO of Deloitte & Touche, a company in an industry that is known for long working hours, thought women quit their jobs to care for their families. He was convinced that this explained why only 10 per cent of partner candidates in his firm were women, but a task force revealed that fewer than 10 per cent left to care for young children. Mothers actually went to work for other firms that would take care of their needs.[76]

In 2004, I was at a dinner in Tokyo with a board member of the company I worked for. During one of the dozen or so courses of a traditional Japanese fine dining, the topic of women at work came up. I do tend to attract these conversations somehow. The board member claimed to be a big supporter of women in the workplace. He said he had, from the beginning of his career, always hired women, 'But then all eight women in my lab started going on maternity leave.' He claimed it was a big staffing problem.

'I have two kids, was on a maternity break, and I'm back at work,' I responded. I explained that with the right mindset and support, it is certainly possible to be a mum and serious about work—and even attend corporate, late-night dinners. He didn't know how to respond. Yet, at the time of our discussion, this was a senior executive who was a board member of a company with 110,000 employees worldwide. His people responsibility was in the tens of thousands, and he was blaming his problems on women and their maternity leave. His dinner comments made me suspect that he even saw women as a liability. Instead, he could have asked: 'What can we do to make it easier for parents to combine having children and careers?' At the time of the Tokyo dinner, he was certainly in a position to act on the answers to that question.

Clearly, there is a leaky pipeline: women voluntarily resign from their jobs at a rate two or three times faster than men once they've been promoted to mid-level leadership positions.[77] They throw in the towel for various reasons. In Europe, across all academic subjects, women account for 59 per cent of undergraduate degrees, but only 47 per cent of PhD graduates and 21 per cent of senior faculty positions.[78]

Is it that women don't want to work when they face childcare issues? Or is the system designed to make it hard for them to work once they have children?

Most people, not just women, seek to balance the various aspects of their lives, including what's best for their family, personal health, self-care, intellectual stimulation, social interaction, financial comfort, and personal and professional growth. As a *Harvard Business Review* article states: 'The pull of child rearing has long been a dominant explanation for the small proportion of women in corporate boardrooms, C-suites, partnerships, and other seats of power.'[79] According to the article, 77 per cent of Harvard Business School graduates overall—73 per cent of men and 85 per cent of women—believe that prioritizing family over work is the number one barrier to women's career advancement.

But do women truly want to prioritize family at the cost of their jobs? A survey of Harvard Business School graduates suggests that at least in elite education, they don't. Male and female graduates have similar values and hopes in their lives and careers but with one decisive difference between the genders. Male graduates expected their careers to take precedence over those of their spouses while the vast majority of women anticipated that their careers would rank equally with their partners.[80] The consequence of this mismatch is evident: it results in women typically taking responsibility for the bulk of the unpaid care and housework and stepping back in their careers.

The authors of the research explained it as follows: 'The vast majority [of mothers] leave reluctantly and as a last resort because they find themselves in unfulfilling roles with dim prospects for advancement.' Men and women are equally ambitious, but men expect to take the lead on the career front. Women expect their career ambitions to be valued on par with men, but that's where they still draw the shorter straw.

Even when women return to work fully committed, they're likely to suffer from the 'mummy penalty' that I mentioned in the previous chapter. The OECD wage penalty for women having children is 14 per cent on average.[81] Upon returning from their maternity leaves, women may be 'mummy tracked', which is the opposite of being on a career track.[82]

'In academia, women have to choose between motherhood and their career,' said my Penn State faculty interviewee. This is creating a gender gap in research in general, which causes further biases when the world is studied from a male lens, as Caroline Criado Perez has proven extensively in her book *Invisible Women*.

Dr Lakshmi Ramachandran agrees. 'They tell you that you don't have to quit,' she said about the advice she received when she wanted to start a family, juggling infertility treatments and career. She felt she couldn't translate the claim 'you can have it all' into action and, after her doctorate in Cell and Molecular Biology, she rejected the opportunity to pursue research at top institutes in the US, including the Massachusetts Institute of Technology. 'I felt I had to choose one or the other,' she shared. 'At least, I didn't feel it within that I had a choice.'

The narrative that women are not committed to their careers is based on a bias that's simply wrong. According to a World Economic Forum paper, women are 10 per cent more productive at work and just as loyal to companies as men.[83] 'Women and men are leaving their companies at similar rates, and they have similar intentions to remain in the workforce,' states the McKinsey Women in the Workplace report,[84] which primarily looks at the US market. It adds: 'remarkably few women and men say they plan to leave the workforce to focus on family.'

Another study noted: 'If women had the same job characteristics and the same percentage with more than one year of experience at the firm, their predicted quit rate would be below that for men.'[85] In other words, women leave within a year when workplaces don't welcome them as much as men, but they stay somewhat longer when they've found the right place. As experienced by Deloitte & Touche, women want the right place that accommodates their needs. Women want a career and are sometimes forced to step back when their partner doesn't, because someone has to take care of the family—whether children or parents.

I've been there myself. During a period when one of our children needed extra attention, I stepped back more than my husband. Someone has to do it, and often the father is less likely to do so because they assume it is not possible, because of a natural assumption that it is the mother's responsibility, or because bosses are not as accepting of fathers stepping back as when mothers do so.

So it isn't that women aren't interested in a career. It's simply that the world makes it difficult for mothers to have a career, and society, companies, and bosses make the wrong assumption that women aren't interested.

As a side note, I do still hear the argument that women are meant to be at home, because it has been that way throughout history. Women would take care of the children and cooking while the men would go out hunting, sometimes for a few days at the time. I'm reluctant to even discuss that in this book, because it is glaringly obvious that the world has changed since then.

Hunting for days is obviously not the most suitable task for women who are pregnant, or recovering from birth, or breastfeeding infants—which women were during an important part of their healthy, adult lives. But if we argue with tradition from the stone age, let's also challenge brushing teeth with a toothbrush and toothpaste. Traditionally, we didn't do this. Of course, this is a nonsensical argument to dismiss the 'women belong with kids' argument. There is no reason to demand that intellectual people focus on family care only today. Superior physical strength is no longer criteria for success at the office. Men have no biological or physical advantage over women in becoming doctors, lawyers, politicians, and CEOs.

From a macro-economic point of view, it is a waste of resources not to employ women. From the viewpoint of seeking optimal conditions for the family, there is no correlation between having a stay-at-home parent and children's future success. There is a correlation between both parents' happiness and children's future success, and intellectual fulfilment is an important factor in people's happiness. The argument that women belong at home because it traditionally was the case is as weak as saying that we traditionally didn't brush our teeth, so we should not do so today.

The system isn't designed to include women with children

Yes, women are likely to quit if they have to choose between a job and the welfare of their loved ones. Men might also do the same if they were forced to choose but they seldomly are; the mummies usually have already given in to the pressure. In order to properly care for children (and sometimes elderly parents), the woman is usually chosen to stay home, both because of traditional roles and because she's likely to be the lower-earning party due to the gender pay gap. This just further exacerbates the pay gap effect, creating a vicious cycle for women, which, like a hamster wheel, they can't escape.

Sadly, the business world simply hasn't been designed to accommodate mothers to the same extent as fathers. Take breastfeeding, for instance. Does your company have facilities for mothers to pump breast milk and safely store it? As Melanie Votaw, one of my editors shared: 'I was floored to see a playpen in a hotel conference room while I was in Japan.' It shows how we can all make a difference to include parents. Even in a country like Japan, where women are often 'retiring' when having children (I'm putting 'retiring' in quotation marks because it is an interesting expression for a Westerner about a thirty-year-old woman—I'm used to people retiring in their mid- or late-sixties).

Nathalie Ricaud was one of a group of very few female managers in her corporation, who wasn't thinking about being provided a room for breastfeeding mothers at the time. 'When I came back from maternity leave, they couldn't accommodate a room,' she says. 'Instead, I found myself with a squeaking pump in a toilet cubicle, terrified that someone might come in. Every time I heard someone enter, I felt I had to stop. It was a lot of pressure, which isn't ideal when you want to pump. I kept going, looking at the big picture. I stored the milk in the staff fridge, which felt awkward. For about three months, I put the milk in a box, so people didn't know.' With that extra awkwardness and pressure, is it a wonder that women sometimes prefer to give up? At the very least, they're often forced to resort to part-time work, especially in countries where childcare costs are high.[86]

In the US, almost two million parents of young children made work-related sacrifices in 2016, according to data from the National Survey of Children's Health.[87] This is against the backdrop of plenty of evidence that women are more likely to remain in the workforce when they get support to balance their needs and the needs of their loved ones.[88] A Sri Lankan study found that there's a positive correlation between job retention and managing job security, working hours, company-leave policy, workload, and employee training in favour of the employee.[89] The OECD report 'Closing the Gender Gap: Act Now' notes that childcare enrolment is growing, and it has enhanced employment of women, whether they work full-time or part-time.[90]

Numerous studies across the globe have shown that when childcare opportunities are increased, mothers seek employment.[1] Conversely, when there are childcare challenges, women leave the workforce: 'More than 2.3 million women have left the labour force since February 2020, accounting for 80 per cent of all discouraged workers during the pandemic, reducing the labour force participation rate to 57 per cent, the lowest it's been since 1988.'[2]

Clearly, it's the system that's the problem, not the women. It's simply time to change the business world, which was designed solely with men in mind. We must make it easier for women to provide their uniquely valuable contributions to the business world, while also remaining human beings who are biologically designed to bear and care for (breastfeeding) children. And mind you, in today's world, there is no reason why men cannot take part and take responsibility in caretaking beyond breastfeeding, or even with feeding infants, if the mother pumps as Ricaud did.

---

[1] For a compilation of research, including evidence that it even is true in African slums, see: Clark, Shelley, Sonia Laszlo, Caroline Kabiru, and Stella Muthuri. 2017. 'Can subsidized early childcare promote women's employment?: Evidence from a slum settlement in Africa.' GrOW Working Paper Series GWP-2017-05 – Research Contribution Paper. https://conference.iza.org/conference_files/GLMLIC_Ethiopia2018_Conference/laszlo_s27717.pdf

[2] Sasser Modestino, Alicia, Jamie J. Ladge, Addie Swartz, and Alisa Lincoln. 2021. 'Childcare is a business issue.' *Harvard Business Review*. https://hbr.org/2021/04/childcare-is-a-business-issue

The benefits of supporting parents through pregnancy and beyond

There is indisputable evidence that the global GDP will increase if women participate in the workforce at a similar level as men. According to a McKinsey study, advancing women's equality would have added US$28 trillion—that's US$28,000,000,000,000,000—to global growth between 2015 and 2025.[91] That would be equivalent to adding the 2015 GDP of the US and China to the world economy ten years later. It would boost global GDP by 26 per cent annually. Other studies similarly show that if the gender gap is eliminated, GDP will increase, such as 12 per cent in Argentina and 9 per cent in Brazil.[92] In India, only 17 per cent of GDP output is generated by women. Imagine if they could add value on an equal footing with men.

Of course, it isn't just country GDPs that will be boosted, the GDP is an aggregation of the value that is added by everyone. Meaning, we will enlarge the pie for everyone, creating market opportunities for the growth of individual corporations too. We'll empower women with financial freedom and give girls, the future generations of women, a better start in life. Daughters of working mothers are more likely to work themselves, have greater financial independence, and are less likely to become victims of violence.

Further, in the US, working parents, employers, and taxpayers experience an annual economic cost of US$57 billion in lost earnings, lost productivity, and lost revenue due to what a report calls the 'nation's childcare crisis'. Businesses alone lose an estimated US$12.7 billion a year due to childcare challenges that their employees experienced even before COVID-19.[93]

Providing better childcare can eliminate these losses.

Organizations benefit from supporting parents through care-phases. A study of data from Australia[94] found that workplaces with on-site childcare and/or family leave policies have lower rates of absenteeism and higher productivity. Barbara Wankoff, KPMG's executive director for diversity and inclusion in 2016, said, 'Paying an additional 10 weeks of salary [for maternity leave], plus the cost of coaching, is much cheaper than paying the equivalent of 78 weeks in [employee] replacement costs (that's 150 per cent of the salary figure).'[95] It's cheaper to support mothers (unfortunately, it is the mothers that are affected rather than the gender neutral 'parents') than to replace them.

The cost of replacing a senior manager can equal up to three times the annual salary and benefits package, according to PwC,[96] and we know that diversity can add 9 percentage points EBIT. There is clearly a business case for retaining employees—in this case mothers.

Scandinavia's 'latte daddies': fathers on paternity leave

'What do you mean, Latte Pappa?' Swedish executive Ville Lumikero asked me when I requested an interview with him on the topic. 'It might have been mentioned in the media when paternity leave started to take off about a decade and a half ago, and it might have lived on in international media. Yes, with the first [child], you might have had the time to pursue hobbies or sit down and enjoy a coffee when the little one is napping, but you can forget about that with the second one. Any "Latte Pappa" glamour quickly evaporates with subsequent babies,' he told me matter-of-factly.

'Paternity leave is just the normal state of affairs now,' Lumikero added. 'It would be a prerequisite for me to take a job to have the standard paternity benefits plus added benefits from the employer.' He's talking about one of the most equal and generous parental-leave systems in the world that allows parents sixteen months of paid leave at about 80 per cent of their salary. Ninety days are exclusive to each parent. In other words, it's 'use it or lose it' for the father and losing it may pose a challenge for the family because childcare for very young ones is more difficult to arrange.

Evidence from Lumikero and his Scandinavian peers shows that real change happens with government regulation. In Sweden, more than 90 per cent of men take paternity leave.[97] The benefits of men taking time off at an early stage are obvious: daddies get to bond with their babies and get used to contributing to child-rearing as their responsibility, too. Scandinavian men contribute on a more equal footing to unpaid care and housework. While Danish men only spend 23 per cent less hours on unpaid work than women do, Japanese men spend 82 per cent less time on cooking, shopping, childcare, and cleaning compared to Japanese women.[98]

'Equality in the workplace will only happen when there is equality in the home,' a Swedish minister said on TV when the 'exclusive parental leave', or 'use-it-or-lose-it paternity leave' began.[99] A 2020 *Harvard Business Review* article titled, 'Gender Equity Starts in the Home', seems to agree.[100] Parental leave for both parents, which seems to result in fathers appreciating the work at home, seems to be an effective step towards equality at home and at the workplace.

Not all societies are committed to a gender-neutral parental leave, though. Ninety countries now offer statutory, paid paternity leave, but the length varies considerably, and less than half of men take advantage of it. So, if gender equality starts at home, fewer than half of men appear to be committed to improving it.[101]

When living in Germany, I had some local friends who were proudly pregnant. When I found out that the father wasn't planning to take paternity leave, I enquired what was holding him back. 'I may as well forget about a career if I would do so!' he replied immediately, highly offended and verbalizing what was clearly a strongly held belief. I tried to convince him that with six weeks of annual leave in Germany, taking two weeks extra once in a lifetime for such an important event surely wouldn't affect his career that badly. He didn't budge in the slightest.

After we both repeated the same arguments a few times, I told him my view as clearly as I could: *He was part of the reason why women, including his wife, weren't taken seriously in the workplace.* 'Imagine what you are contributing to. Your wife is taking a year off, and you're too scared to stand up for your right to take off two weeks to bond with your newborn. Have you ever considered that it's because of men like you that we won't have gender equality in Germany any time soon? Your behaviour is unfair to women, to your wife, and to your unborn child.'

Sadly, our conversation didn't change his decision to not take his paternity leave. We also never saw each other again, marking the end of our friendship. I learned a harsh lesson: If we're going to change the status quo, arguments need to be carefully considered and delivered in constructive ways. The last section of this book is dedicated to advice on more effective communication.

With or without reason, many men are truly afraid of potential career consequences if they do anything different from the norm. The solution is for the government to make it so attractive that a critical number of men will do it. Then, it will become an unquestionable and unchallengeable hygiene factor, as it is in Sweden today.

Lumikero was bolder on the subject. 'Paternity leave is an opportunity for personal development,' he told me. 'You learn things about yourself that you didn't know before.' I agree that parenting teaches us many skills that are valuable at work, particularly in positions of leadership. I certainly learned to get things done efficiently as soon as I had a twenty-minute window granted by the baby's nap, not to mention the persuasion skills, and being both flexible and persistent as the kids get older. And is parental leave perhaps a way to increase men's ability to show compassion and care in the workplace? Could it help them better appreciate unpaid care and continue to take more joint ownership over unpaid care and housework after their paid parental leave is over? Could paternity leave prevent executives from seeing women as a risk simply because they might go on maternity leave?

Regardless of the clear advantages of paternity leave, unfortunately, there are no clear signs that Sweden's practices will bring more women to the top of corporations. The number of female Swedish CEOs is fairly equal to the number of female CEOs in the Fortune 500: seventeen out of Sweden's 289 CEOs are women. Swedish company boards fare better, however, where 33 per cent of board members in listed companies are now women.[102] It's clear that gender equality and inclusion are complex matters. So, while 'use it or lose it' paternity leave may help, it isn't a panacea.

One reason could be that the time given to women is extremely generous: 240 days each.[103] Only ninety are the 'use it or lose it' contingency, and the rest can be taken by the other parent, if both agree.[104] Women still take more maternity leave and end up being away from their jobs for longer time than men, which could end up with the same disadvantages for women in countries without much paternity leave.

Germany is a country that is praised for its family-friendly childcare leave. Three years per child for the first two, and one year for the third. Meaning that women can be away from the office for seven years if they time it well. Of course, seven years is a long time, and in today's fast-moving world, there is a big risk that women pay the price of foregoing their career.

I personally do not find this a particularly family-friendly policy. I have seen plenty of highly educated or otherwise qualified women in Germany who took long childcare leaves, and their skills became obsolete, or they felt uncomfortable working at a level with people almost a decade younger than themselves.

There is no reason for either parent to completely abandon their careers. A study Simon Sinek quoted in *Leaders Eat Last*,[105] demonstrates there is no correlation between a child's well-being and the hours their parents put in at work. The correlation with children's future success is the moods the parents are in when they come home. 'Children are better off having a parent who works into the night in a job they love than a parent who works shorter hours but comes home unhappy,' he quoted. Another study shows that any of the parents' mood after work is positively correlated with adolescent well-being.[106]

Time to let go of mummy and daddy guilt and focus on our personal happiness and fulfilment. Time to be present and have quality time with our loved ones when we are with our loved ones, and pursue our career dreams too.

An expensive myth for both women and organizations

Women lose out when we assume that mothers will take maternity leave and perhaps not even return after pregnancy. As a result, women aren't hired, don't receive training and development opportunities, and aren't promoted. In addition, if we don't value the experience of taking care of children, mum's and dad's pay cheques will differ.

Fortunately, some companies don't see pregnancy as a hindrance to recruiting women. 'I was five months pregnant when I started to look for a job in Singapore and had many interviews,' said Florence Oliveira, currently director of commercial sales at Pinet Industries in Paris. 'I was very surprised to see that the vast majority of recruiters had no issue confirming an interview even after I told them that I was pregnant. My final interview was six weeks after my daughter was born, and I got a job confirmed almost right away.' The unfortunate reality, however, is that globally, Oliveira's experience is the exception, not the rule.

It's highly educated women who have the best chance of correcting the dismal ratio of 7.4 per cent women among Fortune 500 CEOs in 2020, which—fortunately—has risen to 15 per cent in 2022.[107] Yet, these same highly educated women often take more time off when their children are young because they're more likely to have well-paid husbands. Then, when they return from maternity leave and see that men have overtaken them, they lose heart about achieving their previous career dreams. If we don't correct this issue, we'll never achieve gender balance at the top.

The myth that women aren't focussed on their jobs is costing them their careers and costing organizations dearly, since we know that the lack of diversity in leadership means lower profits. Credit Suisse's research has repeatedly found that companies where women made up at least 15 per cent of senior managers have more than 50 per cent higher profitability than those where female representation was less than 10 per cent.[108] As we have shown in this chapter, there are plenty of sound business cases for shattering this myth.

Combatting the myth that women or mothers aren't committed to work

When confronted with remarks that either outright discriminate against women, or simply dismiss them, by implying that they are not interested in a career, here are some of the arguments you can make:

- 'Society seems to believe the narrative that women prioritize children and family over their careers. This isn't true. Research strongly suggests that women want both meaningful work and a career, but it's challenging to combine career and motherhood. Shouldn't we try to solve this underlying problem and ensure there's a career option for all parents?'

- 'Research shows that women stay in their jobs if the environment is supportive, where they can unite their families' need for care with their own desire to stay active in the workplace, even build a career.'

- 'Companies and bosses often claim that women are a liability because they may have children. Women do leave the workforce when it isn't designed to meet their needs, but they stay when it is. Considering the business case for diversity, there's a huge financial upside to making companies equitable for mothers.'

- 'Habits in corporate life have been designed specifically for men. Isn't it about time we reframe our thinking and find out what women need to continue their careers and also have children?'

- 'Companies benefit when mothers continue to work. Studies show that it has a positive effect on the bottom line when organizations make an effort to support women through pregnancy and provide parental leave.'

- 'Besides the fact that gender equality is the right thing to do, supporting female employees though the childbearing and rearing period boosts morale and productivity, attracts talented employees, and reduces the high costs of turnover. All of these factors result in an improved bottom line.'

- 'The myth that women aren't focussed on their jobs is costing them their careers and costing organizations dearly, since we know that the lack of diversity in leadership means lower profits.'

- 'A mindset change is needed. Instead of assuming that women, unlike men, will lose focus at work when they have children, why can't organizations make it possible for all genders to balance life, family, and career?'
- 'Evidence shows that there isn't a penalty for organizations that hire women of childbearing age. Women are at least as loyal to their employers as men.'
- 'We need more paternity leave if women and men are to have more equal opportunities, and various countries have shown it must be a "use-it-or-lose-it" paternity leave. Hiring women will no longer be automatically seen as a liability. For men, it's an opportunity to bond with young children and be more present in their family. They can take on bigger roles in caregiving, and we can let go of the assumption that women can't be leaders because they need to take care of their children.'
- 'Gender equality starts at home. Similar roles and responsibilities in unpaid care and household work, as embodied with mandatory paternity leave, can be enriching for fathers, who can bond with their little ones and increase their emotional quotient. At the same time, it can ease the burden for women, who would no longer have to take on the bulk of the work at home.'
- 'Research suggests that mothers are more productive than their childless sisters.'[109]
- 'Parents often have a great motivation to finish work quickly and, as a result, work more efficiently.'
- 'What can be done for parents to stay on top of trends and developments during their leave?'
- 'We should appreciate the people skills that parents learn while being at home with their children.'

Myth Six

'We Can't Find Women to Fill Leadership Positions'

During an International Women's Day panel discussion, a self-proclaimed staunch supporter of women and supply chain leader for a large company said, 'I would love to promote women into leadership positions, but we simply don't have the pipeline.'

Needless to say, the predominantly female audience didn't receive his comment warmly.

It's scandalous that companies, who have been talking about diversity and inclusion since I entered the workforce as a student intern over three decades ago, still talk about the lack of pipeline. Thirty years seems a more than reasonable timeline to build up a pipeline of female leaders. In fact, give me a fraction of that amount of time, and I'll show you it's more than feasible. It shows that without external pressure with, for instance, quota that come with real punishment, companies don't necessarily change.

Of course, I understand the argument that women haven't naturally gravitated towards STEM careers. This means that fewer women graduate with such degrees, and there's a gender imbalance in the applicant pool. The latest research doesn't find great differences in abilities in, for instance, math,[110] meaning that we will hopefully iron out any gender imbalances in university graduates soon.

While writing this book, I came across plenty of women who left traditional male-dominated STEM jobs because of how they were treated, meaning it is likely that the gender imbalance that we have had in STEM studies is worsened by a toxic work culture and a lack of catering to the needs of women.

Take, for instance, the private hire driver who picked me up from IKEA in Singapore one day. She immediately asked me, 'So what did you buy that you don't need?' I had to laugh because my bag was full of their candles and knäckebröd, but not the footstool I was hoping to get. My driver confessed that she was guilty of the same when she visited IKEA. I'm not sure she ever disclosed her name, so let's call her Danah.

She has a master's degree in engineering and shared that she was tired of how bosses treated her. 'Now, my bosses are the passengers. When they don't respect me, at least I only have to deal with them for twenty minutes. Then, I never have to see them again,' she told me. Danah enjoyed her job running factories, but due to the treatment she recieved, she'll never go back to her original chosen profession.

Consider this: A single mom—rebel at heart, master's degree-holder in engineering, having run production lines for Fortune 500 companies—decided to drive a car for a living because bosses didn't treat her with respect. Isn't it appalling?

While I only know Danah's side of the story, hers is far from the only one. We're losing female talent, including loads of STEM talent, because the business world hasn't been designed with women in mind.

Women are leaving jobs because they don't feel valued, and because they don't feel they fit in.

Back to our supply chain leader. When companies say they don't have a pipeline of female leadership talent, there could be several factors at play:

- They define leadership too narrowly and with labels that are typically seen as 'male' traits, rather than gender-neutral traits. Leadership descriptions frequently use words like 'assertive and analytical, with a go-getter attitude,' which men would more likely relate to than women. They may not even recognize that women can be strong leaders who are focussed, compassionate, and team players.
- They haven't built women leaders. They assume that women don't want leadership positions or that they aren't of the right calibre. As a result, they don't give women stretch assignments, training, or mentoring that is needed to lead large teams.
- They haven't built women's confidence over time that they can one day be leaders. Women typically need more support than men in building confidence to believe that they can hold leadership positions. This is at least partially true because the traditional leadership role model is based on a more 'male' or 'competitive' style rather than the 'collaborative' style that women typically find a better fit. If we can't see ourselves reflected in the current leadership style of others, we dismiss ourselves as future leaders. This means that we don't focus on leadership as a goal, we don't practice it, and we often don't seek to be trained in it.
- They do not make it appealing to women. Often, when women aren't interested, it's because the proposal isn't appealing to them. One example is the frequent requirement to work long hours overtime to be considered effective, committed and 'leadership material'.

Studies show that working over fifty-four hours per week could negate the gains in productivity from working between forty and fifty hours.[111] One study shows that productivity drops when working over forty hours a week. Working sixty hours is less productive than working forty hours.[112] Yes, you read that correctly. Your output is higher when you work forty hours than when you work sixty hours.

Godelieve van Dooren, CEO for Southeast Asia's Growth Markets at Mercer, Singapore, has drawn conclusions from these statistics: 'I tell my team to go home after eight hours. Working more than forty hours per week over a longer period of time is unhealthy and unsustainable,' she said. Van Dooren of course does stress that there are some deadlines that require that extra push, as long as it does not become the rule.

'The biggest and costliest mistakes that I have witnessed happened when people worked crazy hours.' It is also better for diversity, since it will allow those with more unpaid work responsibilities to have a meaningful job and advance in their careers—typically mothers. And back to the 9 percentage points of EBIT advantage of diverse leadership teams, it seems like a logical consequence that it is the better business decision.

In sum, the evidence points towards companies and leaders having failed to build a pipeline. I pointed out to the supply chain leader that I found it odd he hadn't spotted leadership among the women on his team during his three years in that department. I also question HR for not identifying high potential women in other disciplines (such as marketing, where a better gender balance usually persists) for a development path into supply chain leadership.

Leaders often lack the courage to promote people from different industries and functions, with the excuse that the promoted people need 'detailed knowledge' and 'networks'. But as a leader, we primarily need the abilities to lead, listen, and build on expertise. These are cross-function and cross-industry skills. We are leading experts, who have the detailed knowledge that one person cannot possibly have on their own.

To the supply chain leader, I also said: 'How can equity play a bigger role? How can you make sure you give women, and of course each individual in a company, what they need to be successful? And please remember that diversity increases group intelligence. We all stand to benefit from diversity because of the additional perspectives that are brought to the table.'

Perhaps one of the company's men is slightly better for the job, but a woman may be better for the company. Without diversity, a company misses out on the 9 percentage points additional EBIT, as I mentioned in the introduction.

As I've stressed a few times, the business world has been designed by men for men. Take, for instance, Lilian Loh*, an advertising executive. She says she has had a conservative upbringing. Her father still thinks it's better for a woman to stay home, so when Loh was awarded a prestigious award, her father barely acknowledged it.

'I was a stay-home mum for three-and-a-half years, which was great for the family,' Loh says about being a homemaker. 'When the youngest of my four kids was old enough to go to pre-school, I knew I had to go back to work, though.'

Loh knows that she's still the structure that holds the pieces together in her family and 'when things go smoothly, it's okay. It's when something goes wrong that it's very stressful. And sometimes, you don't know that's happening until it's broken,' she said.

She's describing a common situation—the stress that women face from being expected to do more of the unpaid care work at home. Professional women on average do seven weekly hours more of care and housework than men as described earlier. In addition, women typically 'project manage' the entire unpaid work, 'and this takes mental space and energy,' Loh told me.

In general, mothers still take responsibility for keeping up with the kids' emotional and physical well-being, as well as for the shopping, cooking, cleaning, all the extracurricular activities of each child, and on and on. Even when they can delegate some of the tasks, the overall coordination responsibility often falls on their shoulders.

Several women shared the pressure of being the project manager at home in addition to demanding jobs. 'I keep a planner for myself with all critical activities that need my attention. The planner is a mixed planner: it has my work priorities as well as my personal priorities. Everything on one page. I can guarantee you my husband doesn't even have a planner,' says Shalini Pravin, HR Director at Innova Solutions. 'It's my responsibility to know what happens with the children's education, what their extracurriculars are, and what their schedules look like, including who is where and when. My husband will work with me, but he will need me to delegate it and to let him know that he is responsible this time for our second child's weekend plans. And then he will take care of it. But when did he become my delegate?' she asked—rhetorically of course, because we both know that it is considered her inherent responsibility simply because she is the mother.

When society expects us to 'project manage' care and housework, some women won't have the same zest to pursue a stellar career. Fixing attitudes and creating better support systems for families seem like a natural solution.

Real and imagined obstacles

Some of the obstacles to hiring more women leaders are real, while others are imagined.

When looking at female and male candidates on LinkedIn, recruiters are 13 per cent less likely to click on a woman's profile when she shows up in search.[113] The slight good news is that women are 18 per cent more likely than men to be hired after applying for more senior roles.[114] The LinkedIn paper in which this data was published speculates that it maybe because women are more likely to apply for roles when they feel extremely qualified or indicate they are not pursuing stretch opportunities. I believe that this could also be happening because some companies are actively trying to correct past mistakes that resulted in gender imbalances.

In my work as founder of KeyNote Women Speakers, I often hear the complaint, 'I tried to look for a female speaker, but I couldn't find one.' (Note: Please go to keynotewomen.com, as we have a directory full of women speakers.) Yes, some topics are so niche that I have difficulties finding speakers at all, regardless of gender. Like when I was asked to find a speaker for a conference to discuss AI trends in the library industry. But in the majority of cases, I don't find it difficult to find female speakers.

Admittedly, sometimes, women need to be pushed a bit more. We naturally are equipped with less testosterone than men, so there's less of a natural tendency to say, 'I can do this!' I've convinced women to speak by saying, 'Ada, you're a marketing director. One of the speakers is a male senior marketing manager. Of course, your leadership over the department for the past ten years has given you experiences and knowledge that others will be very interested in hearing.' Ada said 'yes', as do most of the other women I nudge, even if I first receive a 'no'.

Sometimes, it's a matter of convincing them that they have worthwhile content, while other times, it's about convincing them that they're inspirational. It helps at times to provide mentoring to increase their confidence, for example by listening to their draft speech and providing tips on how to make it better.

If our professional network consists mainly of men, we may struggle to find a female speaker to fill our speaking slot vacancies. Posting on our male LinkedIn network for a female speaker, for example, may not be as successful as asking someone outside our network who has a profile similar to the one we're looking for. So, it isn't just how we ask; it's also who and where we ask.

It's exactly the same with any other job vacancies. When you look in your male-dominated network (and the language is not as appealing to women, and the recruiter is not trained in listening to how women may describe themselves differently to men), you may not find a suitable female candidate.

Of course, sadly, there are women who don't apply for the reason I mentioned earlier in this chapter. It can be difficult to gather the energy to write an application while working full-time and project-managing everyone and everything in a household.

Some women may also be put off by the wording of a job ad or by other early encounters with the culture at the company in question. When I arrived at a radio station for an interview in Singapore, there was a sculpture in the lift lobby of a huge bird of prey attacking a smaller mammal. The writing next to the sculpture included words about precision and sharp vision, but the larger-than-life statue alone was enough to put me off. To me, it implied that the radio station had a very competitive and aggressive work culture.

Words and symbols matter. They reflect our work culture and if it is aggressive and imposing, more women than men will be put off.

Identity shifts are needed

Herminia Ibarra, Robin Ely, and Deborah Kolb in the *Harvard Business Review*[115] argued that a fundamental identity shift is needed for women to see themselves as leaders, and I agree. Gender bias disrupts the learning cycle that is core to becoming a leader. Women need to see themselves as leaders before they become effective leaders. They state that 'People become leaders by internalizing a leadership identity and developing a sense of purpose.' And how many times have you experienced women dismissing themselves because of the lack of leadership identity? 'Oh, that's not for me,' or 'Other people are much better than me,' are typical ways that the lack of leadership identity expresses itself. Women's expectations of 'being nice' lead to the lack of them exerting authority, and the lack of them speaking up (see p. 35) further exacerbates the situation, as do systemic and human biases. These biases include that we are not seeing the women who are promoted as competent and complain about them landing a certain position just because they are women. And finally, when women are told that it's their fault for not leaning in, although they are frequent victims of being dismissed, it holds many of them back in their careers.

Note that I've left out imposter syndrome as an explanation. Popular coverage on imposter syndrome assumes that it's a female problem to feel persistent self-doubt and anxiety about being exposed as a 'fraud' despite objective successes.[116] Studies, however, show that it's common among both men and women and across a range of age groups.[117] Chamorro-Premuzic is not in doubt: 'The real problem is the imposters, not the ones with imposter syndrome. Having strong humility is not bad. You get better when you listen to criticism, even your own.'

Imposter syndrome is real, but I am not sure whether it is an issue for women alone.

Women possess great leadership skills

Women often take up supporting roles such as human resources, communication and public relations. This means that women are not seen as leaders.

It's comparable to what you'll often see at barbeques. The wife has done the shopping, chopped the veggies for the salad, set the table, and put the steaks out on a tray next to the grill.

The guests come. The man of the house grabs a beer and goes to the barbeque. He serves the guests. The guests marvel at the steaks and the wonderful time and give *him* all the compliments.

Women often take up supporting roles, with the result that we are not appreciated for our contribution, let alone seen as the leaders that we can be.

The reality is that there are plenty of women out there who can lead. As I mentioned in an earlier chapter, a study in *Harvard*

Business Review shows that women outperform men on seventeen out of nineteen leadership skills.[118] Of course, this doesn't mean that men aren't capable of leading, and it equally doesn't mean that all women are good leaders. The research simply proves that there's no reason to keep women out of leadership ranks, and there are leadership competencies that we may have ignored in our organizations.

I must stress this every time I discuss research. Despite women having been told for most of human history that we aren't made for leadership, a study that puts women just slightly ahead of men is seen by many men as a provocation because it doesn't feel good to hear potentially negative generalizations about your entire gender. But this is exactly the point I am trying to make, since the generalizations made for generations about women as an entire gender continue to hold them back in the twenty-first century.

The bottom line is that any gender can produce great leaders, and it will be to everyone's benefit to start looking at leadership in a less myopic way. This will open the gate to a much broader pipeline of talent, not just in terms of gender but also in terms of skin colour, educational background, abilities, and much, much more.

Despite the many discussions on women in leadership training that focus on reverse discrimination, I'm very much in favour of single-gender forums at selected times (to the degree that 'single gender' is still possible in today's world) to ensure women develop their leadership skills. We offer Women in Leadership programmes that boost their confidence in deserving an equal seat at the table, the confidence to lead with their authentic characteristics, and the confidence to speak up at leadership meetings. An all-women environment allows women to find their style of leadership without the dismissal of their beliefs, preferences, and specific challenges.

We have programmes for men as well that focus on how to be more inclusive leaders through allyship and emotional intelligence.

In these groups, it's also easier for them to express insecurities and questions about working with women. For instance, I have had a comment surface more than once from men: 'I'm afraid that I'm promoting so many women around me that there's no more opportunity for me to be promoted.' It's a real fear, and if we don't address it, we won't advance.

This fear is very unlikely to surface in a mixed gender environment. And if we don't address it, the fear will remain with potentially harmful effects to our gender equality goals.

In this case, the argument that addresses the fear is that we're making the pie bigger. By being in the top quartile of diverse leadership, our companies are likely to make 9 percentage points more EBIT than the bottom quartile of diversified leadership representation. By adding more women to the workforce and especially to leadership levels, we add trillions to world GDP, and GDP is a compilation of the value that all organizations add to the economy. When companies and the economy flourishes, there is a place for those who demonstrate real leadership. And inclusion *is* leadership.

Shattering the myth that we can't find women to fill leadership positions

When confronted with the argument that the pipeline is void of women, you can argue:

- 'How long have you had this challenge of not having a pipeline of women leaders?' (Note: This could lead to a discussion about the lack of qualified people in STEM. If not, there's a good chance that the company has simply not put enough effort into ensuring diversity within its ranks.)
- 'What does your company need to do in order to start building a more diverse pipeline?'

- 'How do you define your leadership qualities? Women may lead in different ways than men. Would you be open to the notion that some women on your team may excel at a different set of leadership qualities, including building teams, coaching, collaboration, conscientiousness, patience, listening skills, compassion, empathy, emotional intelligence, and more?'

- 'Are there any women on your team who could be built into strong leaders by providing them coaching or mentoring during their first 100 days, or even for the first year in their new leadership roles?'

- 'Have you looked into why you aren't getting applications from women?'

- 'Tell me exactly, what have you done to ensure that women apply for this position?'
  (Note: The two questions above focus on the underlying root causes rather than assuming women are the problem.)

- 'There are a multitude of reasons why women don't apply, including:
  1. Women aren't attracted to or even put off by competitive or combative wording in the job ads on your website. Collaborative wording often appeals better to women. The same is true for the visual language in ads and even the decor of your office.
  2. The recruiter may have only looked in their own network, which may consist of more men than women.
  3. The company might have defined leadership too narrowly or made the job ad seem too far out of reach for highly qualified women.

- Have you ensured that these three basic criteria for finding a number of diverse candidates have been met?'

Myth Seven

'Women Speak Too Much'

'We want to empower female employees to speak up,' says Shirley Tee, managing director at Bank of Singapore and co-chair for the bank's women's network in Singapore.

Most organizations, such as Bank of Singapore, agree that we need to give women the confidence to speak up. So why are women still perceived to be too talkative? Why do we repeat the myth?

When searching the internet, you can see plenty of sources quoting that women speak 20,000 words a day, while men hover around 7,000 words a day,[3] and I have frequently heard these figures being repeated in social circles.

Digging deeper, as I discovered scientists at University of Penn have done, one of the most likely explanations for these 'statistics' is that a 'marriage counsellor invented this particular meme about fifteen years ago, as a sort of parable for couples with certain communication problems, and others have picked it up and spread it, while modulating the numbers to suit their tastes.'[119]

---

[3] 'New Study Gives Scientific Explanation For Why Women Talk More Than Men.' 2013. *CBS New York*. https://www.cbsnews.com/newyork/news/new-study-gives-scientific-explanation-for-why-women-talk-more-than-men/

In other words, a random figure not based on research turned into a myth, which helped ignite my motivation for writing this book.

I can relate to the speculation that the myth has its origin in couple's therapy. Take the stereotypical breadwinner situation, where the man goes out to work and has intellectual conversations all day, and the woman tends to housework and perhaps children. He comes home and 'has used up all his words'—an argument that sometimes accompanies the above-mentioned figures—or maybe he's just intellectually exhausted. The woman has a big need to have an adult conversation—or any conversation—because she has been conversing with a two-year-old all day. The husband may get annoyed that his wife is speaking too much, and the wife may get annoyed by the husband grunting single-syllable answers.

In 2007, Matthias Mehl of the University of Arizona did his part to shatter the myth that women speak too much. His team counted men's and women's words by recording hundreds of people for several days at a time. The results? Women and men both speak around 16,000 words per day. Women spoke on average 16,215 and men an average of 15,669 words a day. That's less than a 500-word difference or just over 3 per cent difference. In brief, there is no significant difference that can be ascribed to gender.[120]

By contrast, there were large differences around the mean of 16,000 words. The most reticent person was a man who spoke just over 700 words, and the biggest chatterboxes were . . . men, with around 47,000 words daily.

Mehl is quoted as saying: 'What's a 500-word difference, compared to the 45,000-word difference between the most and the least talkative persons?'

The alternative approach: let's speak less and listen more

'We must stop telling women to speak up more,' said Chamorro-Premuzic in his thought-provoking manner when I met him in Singapore. 'We have to stop those from speaking who have nothing to say.'

I agree. Some of my clients have the rule that everyone must speak up in a meeting at least once. Imagine the duplication of content and low relevancy that is built into their meetings. And in Asia, this doesn't work well. Many are reluctant to speak up unless spoken to—it is deeply ingrained in culture. It can be as difficult as a talkative person deciding to not speak any longer.

There is certainly a need for more people to speak up—when you have something to contribute. Preparing your message thoroughly before a meeting and taking the courage to add your parts when it provides added value to the meeting can improve meeting outcomes. However, the advice to ensure you speak up at every meeting is not one I can support.

One collaborator shared with me that he has learned to not say anything in meetings for the first ten–fifteen minutes. He lets other people do the talking. He claims to have been very talkative in the past, but discovered that he was missing out on listening, hearing, and understanding what was truly going on—whether people dynamics, individual agendas, or solutions.

I'm sure it would be a better approach to build a culture where everyone would *listen* in every meeting.

At work, men speak more . . . and interrupt more

Various news sources share a story of how two Uber board members, Ariana Huffington and David Bonderman, jointly attended an Uber all-hands staff meeting. Huffington shared: 'There is a lot of data that shows that when there is one woman on the board, it's much more likely that there will be a second woman on the board.'

She was interrupted by Bonderman, who said: 'I'll tell you what it shows, is that there's much more likely to be more talking on the board.'

What Bonderman demonstrated is that men interrupt women more than the other way around.[122]

Meanwhile, we can find plenty of research and data that shows that men are the talkative ones in professional settings:

- Men spend more time speaking during conference calls.[123]
- Women are reluctant to speak up in mixed or male-dominated environments.[124]
- In groups, men tend to get and keep the floor more often than women, talk more often and for longer, and interrupt more.[125]
- Women speak 75 per cent less than men in most group discussions.[126]
- In one study of meetings, although women composed 46 per cent of attendees, they contributed only 28 per cent of the speaking turns to the average meeting. In only 8 per cent of the meetings from this study were women more likely to speak then men.[127]
- Princeton's women made up 53 per cent of those present at a town hall meeting with the governor, but only 25 per cent of the speakers.[128]

I agree with an article published by Princeton University in which Professor Tali Mendelberg said that gender is one dimension of social inequality, meaning women enter meetings 'with a deficit of authority. They're not taken as seriously. They're not considered as competent. They're not considered to have as much relevant expertise.'[129] It's what Mary Ann Sieghart mentioned in her book, *The Authority Gap*. And this is likely to be true for any under-represented group that doesn't represent the demographic group that typically holds the power. People with different ethnicities, different abilities, or any other under-represented group are much more likely to suffer from a lack of confidence in speaking up.

From my own experience, I can only confirm all the research that says women speak less in professional situations. I frequently do Women in Leadership programmes, and some of my clients want to be inclusive and invite men to sign up too. A mistake, if you ask me. It is shocking to see that as soon as men are participating, women speak less.

In a recent workshop on executive presence that was arranged for women but also allowed men to join, the men spoke more than half of the time. Mind you, there were less than a handful of men in a room of several dozen women. Whenever I asked a question to the room rather than anyone in particular, it was likely to be a man who answered. Men aren't more in the know than women. They are just more confident and probably accustomed to speaking up in a professional situation.

This is one of the reasons why I plead for a safe space for women to find their voices and find the leader within themselves in a single-gender environment. I see it as a key component of developing more female leaders: Make sure they first get the confidence in a safe space, and when they know their power, they can go out and apply their newly-gained leadership confidence.

Culture also plays a big role in maintaining silence. In Asia, children are told by parents, aunties, uncles, and grandparents alike, 'You have two ears, two eyes, and one mouth. Use them proportionally.' As a direct consequence, there are fewer loud voices in most meetings around Asia compared to other parts of the world, such as North America, where the bulk of the research that I have referred to in this book is done. This isn't because I find the US the most important place to focus on; it's just because there is a lack of research on the topic of diversity and inclusion elsewhere. A system-inherent bias, which Dr Laurel Teo, from the National University of Singapore, explained to me was, 'The top-tier academic journals are largely published in the US. As a researcher, publication is a measure of success, and it matters where our research is published. US journals typically have a preference for US data. Therefore, most researchers include US data so that their papers have a greater chance of being accepted in these journals.'

I regularly have clients who ask me to 'teach Asians to speak up'. Of course, I can train people to speak up. However, companies rarely have a well-considered way of managing a culture of speaking up. It starts with accepting that many Asians don't see value in speaking for the sake of speaking. If you are uncomfortable when faced with silence, which is true of most western managers I have encountered in Asia, you fill up the silence with your own words, further discouraging others to speak up.

Radhika Unni, managing director of a leading consulting and IT services company in Singapore, also experienced earlier in her career that companies who urge you to speak up are selective about what you can speak up about. 'In a round table discussion, we were asked what we need to do differently. I mentioned that we don't have sufficient leadership buy-in and that our leadership wasn't strong enough,' she stated in a meeting with mainly peers, but also the head of division. 'I got branded as a loudmouth.'

'I had the fire in my belly to be open and share my view unhindered in a forum with a very senior leader. Today,

I understand that people don't want you to speak your mind. You'll be seen as a problem creator, not as someone who is calling out the right things,' she said.

I know Unni as a sharp leader, who is very measured and diplomatic in a business environment. Was she going too far in that incident, which, as she says, 'created a bit of a scandal?' One leader got fired because of it.

Speaking may backfire for women

'I ask a lot of questions,' Margaret Ann Thomas, currently a realtor in the San Francisco Bay Area, told me. 'It ruined the relationship with my daughter's school when I was the president of my kids' PSP [parent–school partnership] or PTA [parent–teacher association]. I was earnestly asking albeit hard questions, but that was not welcome.' She said that women, especially mums, are always going to ask harder questions. 'They're always going to be more curious. It's the nature of our own ability to self-reflect. I don't want to say that women think through things better, but we see five steps ahead. It's the anticipation of watching your kid fall down the stairs. You're constantly in anticipation mode. I think that's a natural instinct that occurs in women.'

'Would the school have been more open to your challenging questions if you had been a man?' I asked her. She didn't flinch and answered, 'There is a big gender line in how our school manages mums versus dads.'

In other words, yes. She experienced that she was perceived as annoying because she asked difficult questions that could have created a better school.

Research confirms this. One study comparing the fictitious bios of female and male CEOs shows that the women, when speaking more than the average person, received lower leadership ratings, while the opposite was true for male CEOs. If they were talkative, men were ranked as the better leaders. In fact, men were perceived as better leaders in general—regardless of how frequently they spoke.[130]

Another study shows that men get credit for voicing ideas, although not when voicing problems. Women don't get credit at all—neither when voicing ideas, nor when voicing problems.[131] Both Unni and Thomas may have been affected by this. We don't want women to speak their minds. We can speak up as long as we agree to what's said. 'But please don't rock the boat.'

'Every time I said something that didn't agree with the men in the room, I would get comments such as "oh, she is getting saucy," or "she's getting upset again,"' Malaysian Aarathi Arumugam says about her time working in the UK as a financial director in a male-dominated environment.

'I haven't been told that I speak too much, but I have heard it said about me. It was fairly early in my career. I drew back and became measured before I spoke,' she shared. 'Now, I am told I don't speak enough. I am told I am a snob because I don't say anything unless I am going to be listened to.'

I was curious how she would know when she would be listened to. 'Exactly,' she said as she burst out laughing, clearly making her point that we must put a much bigger effort into our feedback to women, who suffer from the double bind. In this case, you're too talkative or too snobbish. No sweet spot in the middle seems possible for women.

'I've been told I talk too much, but now that I am in a senior leadership role, nobody will tell me this to my face,' Priyadarshini Sharma, a senior leader told me. 'They will say that very casually about other women, though. It's all about how we are nurtured. We've been told as children, "Girls should be seen and not heard," right? And "Good girls don't talk too much." Both genders are affected by it at the workplace. Women don't share their opinions and have to be called upon to speak. And the guys? They speak—even if it is just repeating what's on the agenda.'

'And when women speak, people do not listen.' She confirmed that 'bropriation' is a real thing at the office: Women say something; nobody pays attention. The guy repeats it, amplifies it, and gets the credit. Then, everyone says it's a great idea.

A female leader that I spoke to, Pooja Iyer*, took me back to a previous job in her native India. She was the only woman in the room. 'We're having this conversation about the next campaign for a microwave where I suggest targeting women and lay out my plan on how to do it. Then, the men start saying that we need to target the husband, because they are the decision-makers around buying appliances. Comments that make it so obvious that they have little insight into consumer behaviour fly across the tables such as, "Microwaves are the lazy women's alternative." They are not respecting any of the research that I did to find out what is needed for a successful campaign. The only way that I could get past their misogyny and ageism was to keep getting back to data, keep getting back to facts, keep getting back to actual information so that it's not just about personal opinion. Even though I was equally qualified, even though I had done all the research, it was just about their viewpoints. I had to make a lot of concessions to get my campaign through,' she said. As a highly educated and experienced marketing manager, Iyer felt the 'double whammy' of being a woman as well as younger than the peers around the table.

Later, she got an extra whammy, when she worked for western companies that would have very white boardrooms. She left one company because she knew she could neither break the glass nor the bamboo ceiling.

The next time I met her, she told me a story that made my jaw drop: 'When I worked at a fast-moving consumer goods company, men in the feminine care department would walk around with sanitary pads to get the customer experience.' I believe it needs no further explanation why this shocked me. Diversity increases group intelligence because we bring in different perspectives. This again nurtures creativity and innovation. And what this feminine care department ignored at that time: You are more likely to be successful when your employees reflect the make-up of your customers. A focus group can never replace the deeper understanding that you will have about your consumers when you employ them and make them responsible for product development and marketing.

One thing that stands out in my conversation with these dozens of highly qualified and highly accomplished women is their 'humility' that borders putting themselves down and placing men on a pedestal. Women typically see themselves as less qualified when they compare themselves with others. When sharing her story of discussing the microwave campaign with colleagues, Iyer referred to her skills with 'even though I was equally qualified . . .' She has an MBA from a top institution, fifteen years of marketing experience working for big brands, and was the microwave marketing expert in the room. As with so many of the women I speak to, they play down their talent, competencies, and experience. Iyer was the expert in the room in all relevant aspects, and yet, described herself as 'equally qualified'. She was the expert and *higher* qualified; yet the men in the room didn't listen. And she put herself down.

'Good catch,' she said about my observation that she played down her qualifications. 'Think about it, though. God forbid if I ever say that I am more qualified than someone. If a woman says that, she is arrogant. She's got a big head. There's not a humble bone in her body.'

I began to understand why women are considered as speaking too much. It's because others in the meeting don't want to hear us. If what is said makes someone uncomfortable—for whatever reason—anything that is being said is too much.'

A female board member from a double-digit multinational organization who wants to remain anonymous confirmed this. 'It's irritating to have me on the board because I question a lot of the decisions,' she shared with me in confidence.

Sharesz T. Wilkinson, executive communication expert, explained it as the difference between deductive and inductive thinkers. 'It's not so much a gender issue as a deductive versus inductive communication approach,' she said. 'It's about being a powerful communicator with the right tone of voice, to pacing, to volume and choosing the right words, and tailoring a message.'

Deductive thinkers need to hear the main point you are making first. The details can then be added later. Inductive thinkers need context first, which may be seen as unimportant details by the deductive thinker. The inductive thinker is often seen as long-winded by the deductive thinker.

It's similar to the differences in how we structure a message in different cultures. The Anglo-Saxon education system focuses very much on first saying the main message followed by supporting points. East Asian culture typically focuses on painting a picture and providing the context, from which conclusions can be drawn, often even indirectly (see p. 203).

Bullying: when criticism goes too far

I shared my hypothesis that women speak differently rather than too much, which is seen as 'being difficult', with Jessica Hickman, founder of Bullyology and author of *The Upstander Leader*. She added that there is a lot of insecurity around women who are too powerful. 'That's when others start saying that they speak too much and pull them down,' she said. 'When I presented in the boardroom, my boss would make dismissive comments and ultimately diminish what I said or even get up and leave the room pretending to take a call or attend to something deemed more important than me.'

Hickman worked in the oil and gas industry at the top end of Australia and was awarded for her work. It infuriated her manager, who was vocal about the need for women to be seen and not heard. 'He believed that I was only successful because of the way I look rather than my skillset. It knocked my confidence [down],' she told me. This is the devastating part about the myths we retell over and over again. We risk breaking women's confidence, which already suffers compared to men's. It's a vicious cycle, where women are then not hired for leadership positions because they don't speak up and show less confidence than men.

'I reported this thirty-two times to upper management,' Hickman says. 'I was told, "Toughen up princess, it is the industry," "Don't be so emotional," "You look fine on the outside," "You're confident, just ignore him." And time upon time again, I would go through the emotional roller coaster with no support.' With Hickman, it went as far as bullying, which she has described in her book.

Media often portrays women as shrill, unreasonably emotional, and talkative. Just look at the women on many reality shows such as Netflix's *Dubai Bling* for example. In the show, high society women are portrayed as more emotional, talkative, and hysterical. Even in shows where it's the man who speaks more, he isn't likely to be portrayed as a chatterbox, like a woman might be.

Women do naturally have higher pitched voices, but when people are disempowered from speaking up, their voice may become more strained, less confident, and even shriller. Sharma and I have both worked on our voices to get more volume and power, and Sharma also practised slowing down. 'I think very fast, and I naturally speak very fast. Taking pauses and improving my cadence is something I've learned,' she said.

Of course, perhaps by bad luck, I have come across a few 'undiplomatic' women who have gone too far. But why then would I constantly meet women who are told they have gone too far simply because they spoke up? I've mentioned my own experience of challenging the pay gap and subsequently being told I'd gone too far. I'm convinced that many company cultures aren't ready to listen to diverse opinions because of the additional effort required to address the issues.

Creating a true culture for everyone to feel safe in speaking up needs active work, according to a senior executive from a large food company I spoke to. 'Inequalities and discrimination can prevent marginalized groups from feeling comfortable enough to voice their opinions and ideas,' he shared with me. 'The desire for conformity and a need to conform to the status quo can also make it difficult for individuals to speak up and challenge the norms.' In other words, marginalized groups suffer from not being included and may focus on not rocking the boat. The result is a lack of diverse voices and opinions.

Back to Shirley Tee, who said she wants to get women to speak up to further gender diversity in leadership. Certainly, how much you speak is important if you want to be seen as a leader. The 'babbly hypothesis' is backed by research. It says that there's a strong correlation between speaking time and whether you are considered a leader.[4]

---

[4] For a confirmation of this hypothesis, see:

MacLaren, Neil G., et al. 2020. 'Testing the babble hypothesis: Speaking time predicts leader emergence in small groups.' *The Leadership Quarterly, 31*(5), https://www.sciencedirect.com/science/article/pii/S1048984320300369

I do want to question whether the same effect (quantity of speaking, not its quality, determines leader emergence) is true across cultures. I have a hypothesis that it will be less pronounced in Asia compared to the US, where the aforementioned study was conducted.

Shattering the myth that women speak too much

When confronted with the accusation that women speak too much and too much nonsense, you can help change the narrative by saying:

- 'This is a deep-rooted myth. Research shows there is no significant difference between men and women. Both genders speak around 16,000 words per day. On the other hand, in meetings, men take the floor more often and for a longer time, interrupt more, and speak longer on earning calls and at conferences. In any professional situation that has been researched, men talk more and seem in general to have worse speaking etiquette than women.'

- 'Please consider that women who speak up—whether for pointing out a problem or proposing a solution—are punished for doing so. How can we create a more inclusive culture where our perception of women speaking too much is changed to women having different perspectives that should be heard and supported?'

- And, as always, our gender-perspective swapping comment: 'Would you have described her as too talkative if she were a man?' Or, 'How would you have described her if she were a man?'

- If they are still suffering from the impression that someone spoke too much, consider reverting to the facts. For instance: 'She spoke for a few minutes and was the only woman who spoke during a one-hour meeting.' Or, 'Yes, she could have gotten to the point a bit faster. As could have Jack, Joe, and John.'

Myth Eight

'Women Bosses Are Too Bossy'

'Ever since I was six years old,' Margaret Ann Thomas told me when I asked whether she had ever been told she was bossy. 'And I'd like to say I'm assertive.'

Sheryl Sandberg, author of *Lean In*, a book that started a global women's empowerment initiative of the same name, launched a campaign to ban the word 'bossy'. 'Ban bossy'[132] increased awareness around the world that when a little boy asserts himself, he's called a leader. Yet, when girls do the same, they're often branded as bossy, or 'always telling people what to do', as the Oxford dictionary defines the term. Bossy clearly has a negative connotation.

'Being bossy is a controlling mechanism that we use to get other people to do what we want in a way that doesn't come from a place of kindness or nurturing, but selfishness,' Thomas told me. 'We use it when girls and women ask for what we need and want. It's not bossy if we do it with kindness and love. We just have to change the language for that.'

Thomas's daughter goes to a school in California that is quite left leaning. She said, 'I can't believe that they don't address more of this in schools. They teach racism and genocide but not enough about gender equality. They are not even taught the word "misogyny" and staff do not address the girl dynamics that are going on in the playground,' she lamented.

I've been on both sides. I've called my daughter bossy once or twice. I have a boy and a girl, and I don't think I have ever called my son bossy. I can assure you that they both have strong minds. Clearly, I'm as biased as the rest of the world. I quickly corrected myself, but the damage was done. My daughter immediately knew I meant something negative when I said she had executive potential. It's so deeply ingrained in our culture that we see girls as bossy at the first sign of them being stubborn.

On the receiving end, I've been called bossy. Of course, I am indeed the boss of my company. I have the financial responsibility, and while I welcome input from everyone on the team, I'm the one who will bleed when wrong choices are made. So, if I believe a proposal won't work, I won't pay anyone to implement it.

I'm not bossy. I'm the boss. I have my own money in the game.

Thomas shared a story from her production days when she was called bossy by one of her designers. 'It got to a point where I stopped asking her to work. I knew I couldn't make any comments, criticism—nothing about her design.'

'*Were* you being bossy?' I asked her.

She paused and reflected. 'In the beginning, I think I was bossy. I wasn't mindful of who she was. Like, I wasn't really seeing her. And maybe she felt threatened and became defensive. And angry. All of that because I didn't listen, and I didn't understand her fear. It was a great lesson for me.'

After another pause, she added: 'I'm having a bit of a therapy moment with you,' and burst out laughing.

I could have left it at that and taken it as proof that she was bossy. My experience of asking one question meant that the story was not immediately brushed to the side. The question was: 'Would you have been described as bossy if you were a man?'

'No! No, no, no! No way!' she said energetically, bursting out laughing again.

Women are described as the bossy ones

Alyssa Goh* had just left the financial industry where she held a position as executive vice president when I caught up with her over tea in Singapore.

Just as with all senior, confident, and accomplished women I'd asked whether she'd ever been called bossy, Goh said without hesitation, 'Oh, yeah, I'm the bossy one.' She summed up the detailed feedback when she was told she was bossy as: 'She is not collaborating; she doesn't listen; she only wants to tell; she doesn't work well; it's her way or the highway.'

In 360 reviews, peers, global colleagues and superiors always confirmed that she was seen as a highly collaborative person. While she shared her entire story, I became convinced she's an assertive executive, committed to doing the right thing. She didn't want to get involved in financial decisions that were unsound and clearly driven by politics. A few of the other senior female leaders were on her side too.

'Were you called bossy because you weren't playing to his personal agenda?' I asked, referring to the big boss, making sure that I didn't run the risk of misunderstanding what was already obvious to me.

'Yeah,' and she gave me the analogy of the emperor's new clothes. 'I'm simply calling out that he wears no clothes.'

'I don't think female bosses are bossier,' Shirley Tee from Bank of Singapore told me. 'It all boils down—whether male or female—to whether they are having insecurities or not. Do you have enough confidence to be a leader and to really lead the team? If you feel insecure then there's a chance that you can come across as being bossy because you want to stand firm. You want people to really follow your rules, and then you may become very bossy.'

If this is true, a logical conclusion is that the risk of women becoming bossy is higher because they feel less confident.[5] If we tell women that they aren't born leaders, make them feel like they don't fit in because the business world has been designed with men in mind, or make them feel they have to assert themselves constantly, they may resort to telling others what to do in a pushy way in an effort to be controlling.

At the same time, we know that women are called bossier more often than men, and we're more likely to connect the term to women and girls than to men and boys.[133] Tee disagreed with this perception. 'Being bossy has nothing to do with the gender. It's down to the individual's personality—male or female,' she said.

Can bossy become a positive attribute?

Some voices urge us to *claim* the word bossy. 'Perhaps we should teach girls to embrace the word "bossy" to channel their bossiness into productive methods of leadership instead of being hurt when someone calls them it.' *Time* magazine suggests this in an opinion piece. 'We should encourage girls to accept themselves for who they are, to be proud of their strengths, even if the boys in the

---

[5] For a great overview of studies done to demonstrate this, see: Kay, Katty, and Shipman, Claire. 2014. 'The Confidence Gap', *The Atlantic* https://www.theatlantic.com/magazine/archive/2014/05/the-confidencegap/359815/ (Accessed on August 7, 2023)

classroom or the men in the boardroom try to undermine us by spinning those strengths into something negative.'[134]

Author Adam Grant, who overall has great perspectives on many things, has what I see as a white male perspective on this: 'When young women get called bossy, it's often because they're trying to exercise power without status. It's not a problem that they're being dominant; the backlash arises because they're overstepping their status.'[135] This completely ignores the fact that we don't call little boys bossy as often as girls and that we don't encourage the assertive behaviour of girls. Instead, we encourage them to be 'nice'. Back to when I called my daughter bossy, she clearly perceived it as negative, and this can very quickly discourage her from being assertive and even hinder her from seeing herself as leadership material.

The Center for Creative Leadership has done the needed homework. 'Bossy' is a negative term, they have found, and it's being used to label women's behaviour twice as often as men's behaviour.

The study respondents defined 'bossy' as those who:

- control others and dictate orders;
- ignore others' perspectives;
- are rude and pushy;
- micromanage and prescribe specific actions (for e.g., saying exactly how or when something should be done);
- focus on authority, power, and status; and
- interact in aggressive ways.[136]

Again, women are held to higher standards: bossiness hurts women more than men, the study showed.

In a 2014 *Wall Street Journal* article,[137] Sheryl Sandberg and Ann Maria Chávez argued that the word 'bossy' isn't just a playground insult. I'm so fascinated by the facts that I feel compelled to repeat them here:

- 'The first citation of "bossy" in the *Oxford English Dictionary* refers to an 1882 article in *Harper's Magazine*, which declared: "There was a lady manager who was dreadfully bossy."'
- 'The use of "bossy" to describe women first peaked in the depression-era 1930s, when popular sentiment held that a woman should not "steal" a job from a man, and reached its highest point in the mid-1970s as the women's movement ramped up and more women entered the workforce.'
- 'Most dictionary entries for "bossy" provide a sentence showing its proper use, and nearly all focus on women. Examples range from the *Oxford Dictionary*'s "bossy, meddling woman" to *Urban Dictionary*'s "She is bossy, and probably has a pair down there to produce all the testosterone." Ingram shows that in 2008 (the most recent year available), the word appeared in books four times more often to refer to females than to males.'

Shattering the myth that women are too bossy

When confronted with the argument that women are bossy, you can help change the narrative by saying:

- 'Would you call her bossy if she were a man?'
- 'If a man had behaved in the same way, would you call him bossy?'
- 'Why do you think she needs to be "bossy" to do her job?'
- 'Let's ban "bossy". Let's not describe women as bossy, pushy, b****, or catty when they are simply asserting themselves.'
- 'I'm bossy because I'm the boss. I'm telling you what to do because that is my responsibility.'
- Ask them to describe the behaviour in more detail than 'bossy': 'What specific behaviours do you mean by "bossy"?'
- Make sure to bring your argument to the end, for e.g., 'Sounds like she is being assertive.' Or, 'Sounds like she is ensuring that the investment has a high ROI(return on investment).' Or, 'Sounds like that would be a positive trait if a man were described like that.'
- Or suggest solutions such as interpersonal skills training if the issue is stemming from a lack thereof.

Myth Nine

'Women Are Indecisive'

As a reminder of how little we use logic in our judgement of women, the myth that they are indecisive must follow the chapter on women being too bossy. Since 'bossy' usually entails wanting to decide everything, how are we also indecisive? Isn't this the double bind at play again?

There is a strong myth surrounding women's indecisiveness. *The New York Times* puts it aptly: 'Women may be seen as indecisive, encumbered by their need to build consensuses, weighted down by a lack of self-confidence and an inability to handle stress.'[138] In a study by the US-based Pew Research Center, three times as many respondents saw decisiveness as a masculine rather than feminine trait.[139]

Female leaders see this differently, though.

'We're good at making decisions. We know we have twenty minutes to prepare dinner, we take one look at the fridge, see what's available, and we know what is needed to feed the kids,' Sharma told me. She explained how this transcends decision-making at work as well: 'Women look at "what's the job to be done" and "this is the time available", "these are the resources", and they know what is good for people. And women don't have much time. We get everyone aligned very quickly and move on with it and execute it.'

She shared a leadership principle that shows her preference for deciding quickly: 'An okay strategy executed brilliantly is better than a brilliant strategy never executed. And that's the idea about execution. Understand the issue and what's going on, connect the people and the dots, and then take that decision.' She touched upon a point that most experts and studies agree on: the people element features more strongly in women's decision-making process.

'We are used to managing multiple things—family, career, fitness, social life, and so much more—so we just get on with it. We take the decisions. There's no time for anything else,' she told me during one of our meetups.

Women and men decide differently

A *Harvard Business Review* article discusses how women who decide on purchasing decisions in corporate life do have different criteria compared to men. 'Women see a meeting with a candidate service provider as a chance to explore options in collaboration with an expert resource, while men see that event as a near-final step in the process when they are narrowing down and choosing among options,' it states. 'And whereas male buyers expect head honchos to be present at the meeting, female buyers are more interested in talking to the people they will actually be working with.' In addition, 'women are inclined to be more inquisitive, wanting to hear everyone's thoughts before deciding. They spend more time finding the ideal solution.'

Women are *not* less decisive than men. The way different genders take decisions does show different tendencies, though. Therese Huston explored this in her book, *How Women Decide,*[141] and mentioned two areas where women and men decide differently. Women are more analytical rather than intuitive and not as affected by over-confidence as men.

Women are more analytical; men more intuitive in decision-making

Against our gut feeling that women are more intuitive, Huston says that women are not more likely than men to take a decision based on intuition alone. In fact, women are more analytical than men in decision-making. Women are more likely to draw on facts and do their research than men.

Note that including a gut feeling in a decision may also be healthy if we see 'gut feelings' as a collection of experiences and knowledge stored in our subconscious mind. We sometimes 'know' without being able to pinpoint what makes us feel convinced. It's our brain's way of effectively storing knowledge so that our conscious mind doesn't get overloaded. However, 'gut feelings' can also be a subconscious bias that is coming up and avoiding the unknown, or avoiding people who are different from us. In such cases, looking at the facts is naturally the better option.

One study went into more detail in finding that women are less likely to be intuitive decision-makers and more likely to involve others. The authors suggest that their study may indicate that men are *more impulsive* in decision-making. As an interesting sidenote, the older we get, the more likely all of us are to take on the female profile of being more analytical and involving others in decisions.[142]

Confidence and over-confidence

Confidence is another factor that can stand in the way of good decisions. This is true for all genders. As Chip and Dan Heath describe in *Decisive*, over-confidence about the future may come in the way. With men leading on the confidence scale, this could be an impediment for decisions because over-confidence can easily become harmful in decision-making. For daily decisions that don't have wide-ranging negative impacts, taking a decision rather than not taking it is our better option, because not taking a decision is also a decision. However, for larger business decisions, controlled risk appetite based on facts is better. Over-confidence can cloud this, as Huston shared.

A former business partner shared a story with me about a room filled with parents. The speaker asked, 'Who is an expert on breastfeeding?' None of the women, who all had children and presumably had provided both of their breasts to their children for months, raised their hands. One man raised his hand immediately, saying, 'I've observed my wife doing it.' That was enough for the man to have the confidence to call himself an 'expert', while actually doing it did not make the many women in the room confident enough to label themselves as such.

Men systematically estimate their intelligence higher than women do, as a 2022 research paper published in Australia has again shown.[143] There is no correlation between gender and intelligence, but men tend to think they're smarter than they are to a much larger extent than women: 8.5 IQ points in this study. In fact, it goes beyond gender. 'Masculine and androgynous subjects reported higher general self-esteem scores than feminine and undifferentiated' research participants. This phenomenon has been dubbed 'male hubris, female humility'. Males have higher self-esteem, and with that self-esteem bias, which leads us to evaluate ourselves consistent to our self-esteem, men believe in their competence more than women do. And this can lead to over-confidence, and impulsive and rash decisions.

Including important stakeholders

One study has found that women on boards achieved significantly higher scores in 'making consistently fair decisions when competing interests are at stake'.[144] In other words, keeping both the interest of the business as well as considering the viewpoints of various stakeholders. Including different perspectives, being cooperative, building consensus, rallying support, and focussing on fair and moral decisions that benefit more stakeholders are some of the characteristics they found more pronounced in the women in the study.

All of this is despite the fact that women's missteps typically have more severe consequences for them than men's missteps have for them. It actually wouldn't be surprising if women were more reluctant to make decisions after they've seen other women suffer disproportionally for decisions that didn't turn out well.

Men have the added advantage that their decisions are more readily accepted as being what must be done—even the hard, unpleasant ones. It's what Sieghart has written in *The Authority Gap* as mentioned earlier in the book, in which she illustrates that we take men more seriously than women. Women have to prove their competence, whereas with men, we are more likely to take their competence for granted. This is still the case although we have seen female world leaders react swiftly against the backdrop of the emergence of the COVID-19 pandemic.[145] Women country leaders were the ones that took quick, decisive action after seeking advice from various stakeholders, including medical experts.

In 2023, two female prime ministers announced their resignations within one month. Jacinda Ardern of New Zealand was followed by Scottish Nicola Sturgeon about four weeks later. There was a lot of discussion about the decisions, which immediately focussed on gender and included the notion that they 'gave up' too easily. Luckily, there were also plenty of voices that called it a positive move, describing it for instance as 'graceful'. I agree that these were brave decisions that bore in mind the interest of the country as well as other stakeholders and not least themselves. They had both been long-serving prime ministers, and the decision to step down in time is, in my view, a sound one that many other leaders could learn from.

Stress

Women have been told they're unpredictable and can't take good decisions when under stress. The widespread narrative is that women cannot deal with stress. However, the argument that men fare better under stress doesn't seem to hold. There is no significant difference between genders according to a 2022 study.[146]

Huston provides ample evidence that this narrative is unfounded, and her compilation of evidence suggests that the opposite is truer. She stated that women tend to become more strategic under stress, looking for smaller, sure successes rather than risky prospects. Huston quoted a study that stresses the point. When people were asked to inflate virtual balloons in a computer game, men made riskier decisions. You can press the pump key to inflate your balloon with money, but at some point of time, your balloon bursts. Just like in *Who Wants to be a Millionaire*, you can collect the money at any point of time. But you also lose everything if you make the balloon explode—and that can happen at any given time. Women and men performed similarly when everything was calm. However, when they added a bit of stress—in the lab simply immersing a hand into water just above freezing point—women were more conservative. Men pumped the balloon 50 per cent more often, meaning they took a bigger risk[147]. In this study, men cashed in greater rewards because they took greater risks, but you can imagine many situations where an all-risk approach is not helpful. The only risks were not winning money, where in real life situations, taking a risk that has greater pay-outs may lead to irresponsible risks in other areas too. And whether risk is positive or negative, of course, depends on the business and the situation.

Another study found that a group of men would more often go for an all-in approach, for e.g., when deciding on corporate strategy, whereas when women are involved, a moderate path would be more likely to be chosen.[148]

I don't find it hard to believe that some stressed men tend to suffer from questionable decisions when the stress ramps up, risking a lot for the slim chance of a big win. We are all aware of stories that support this.

Nick Leeson is a banker who became famous overnight for gambling away $1.3 billion for Barings Bank in 1995. Risk is part of the game in trading, although, in this case, the damage was aggravated because he deceived his bosses and hid his losses.

We thought the industry had taken a lesson from the incident until Jérôme Kerviel pulled a similar stunt, only six times as big a loss for his employer, Société Générale. Anxiety and stress could have led both men to make bad calls.

You may also remember how US energy giant Enron's downfall was caused by the revelation of massive losses—billions of dollars—that had been hidden in a myriad of special purpose vehicles. The management team was all male, and benefitted personally from a high share price, which was an 'obsession' of theirs.[149]

Calculated risks—not the impulsive or reckless ones, but the ones we need to take in business when we don't have all the information available—is another area where women could benefit from improving their image. Men underestimate the likelihood that women will take risks, according to Huston and as we have seen above.

Categoric thinking

'Men tend to organize the world into distinct categories whereas women see things as more conditional and in shades of grey,' an article in *Scientific American* said.[150] Interestingly enough, the article stated that there's no difference between gender in how confident we are about the decisions we have taken. We put the same dose of trust in our judgement.

Moral judgement

In situations that need moral judgements, men tend to rely on principles of justice, duty, and fairness that apply universally. Women more strongly emphasize the specific relationships between people and the situation.

Decision-making isn't just a single skill. It involves many skills from clarifying priorities, coming up with options, analysing and testing these, selecting the best option, getting a buy-in, preparing plan B in case something goes wrong, and seeing it through. There are strong individual and cultural variations.

My husband and I: a male–female comparison

I can be very fast in taking decisions, which, as an entrepreneur, I have learned to do. Having worked for a company with a very risk-averse culture, I had to develop a greater appetite for risk. If there is an opportunity or threat to your business, you must respond quickly.

I left corporate life a handful of years before my husband did, and I could tell how it shaped me in deciding fast and taking controlled risks. I don't have the luxury to think about minor details for a long time. I agree with Sharma that with a lack of complete information, it's less effective to postpone a decision too long rather than to take a decision that may prove less favourable. Planning and pondering for too long will have opportunity costs in terms of loss of income.

I also know from experience that when we put all our ducks in a row to make something happen, the action itself means we're already moving closer to our target. If we fail, we deal with that when it happens. The risks in my business aren't bigger than my confidence so I can master whatever comes my way. I've already been through a two-year pandemic that pulled the carpet from under my feet.

I'm a lot more intuitive in my decisions than my husband. I don't ignore information; I'm definitely analytical and trust facts. The evidence is in the research upon which I have based the book you're reading right now. At the same time, I know that intuition is a collection of experiences, and if I walk into a house that feels good, my husband will come to a very similar conclusion when he uses his Excel sheet in the same decision-making process of finding a new place to rent, for example. We've barely disagreed on any of the decisions to be made on where to move despite our very different approaches to reach the conclusion. And we have moved dozens of times.

We further differ and call them decisions with a Big D or small d, inspired by Erin Meyers in *The Culture Map*.[151] When he takes a decision, it's a Big D Decision. That's what we're going to do. My decisions are small d decisions. It's a decision until the situation changes, a more interesting option pops up, or I feel differently about it, which can be frustrating for someone who has taken a Big D Decision. This may be the reason why a *Harvard Business Review* article[152] says that women are discovery-oriented decision makers. We can accuse women of being 'prone to changing their minds', or flexible and adjusting to a new situation or options that have appeared. For those tending to take Big D Decisions, of course this can result in frustration. Take, for instance, a man who was quoted saying 'I think sometimes women are so much more difficult, and even fickle, in business dealings,' in that same article.

It can be gender, and it is partly cultural, just like my husband has a more typical German view of decision-making.

As a result, I don't believe it's black and white that a single gender is better at decision-making. But if we go back to the list of leadership skills in which women outperform men,[153] there's one thing I'm very sure about: There's no reason why women should inherently be any less decisive than men.

Ensure everyone is included in the decision-making process

In some patriarchal societies, women still need a signature from a man to receive reproductive healthcare.[154] In even more countries, women need the signature of their husbands to set up a company or take up employment. Socialization means that girls and women often follow the will of their father. However, even when socialization means some women are out of practice with decision-making, they are inherently as capable as men to do so. It's simply that we tend to have different ways of going about it.

Many women have been used to doing things differently than men. When someone does things differently, such as reflecting on what are considered unusual points, basing it on different principles, and following different processes, it can seem annoying to those who have become used to the status quo. As with the narrative that women speak too much, anything that's different may seem like 'too much' or, in this case, the 'wrong' approach.

Whether women are decisive or not is not even the most relevant question. We know that increased diversity leads to smarter decision-making. Numerous studies, including Deloitte's 'Women in the Boardroom' report[155] have concluded this. Meaning, decisions are better when we have diversity in the room which women often can bring along. The report further states that implementation of decisions is smoother when there is diversity—simply by increasing buy-in and trust.

If we want to aim for greater, more holistic outcomes, women are needed in the decision-making processes at the workplace. Women must be represented in all walks of life—as must men—including in leadership roles where key decisions are made. Whether in senior leadership or on boards, in schools and academia, politics, and government, it's essential to have good gender distribution.

Shattering the myth that women are too indecisive

When confronted with the argument that women are indecisive, you can help change the narrative by saying:

- 'Women and men are equally capable of sound decision-making. They simply go about it in different ways.'
- 'She isn't capable of taking a decision because she has a lack of competencies in the field. It has nothing to do with gender.' And, 'What training and exposure does she need to compensate for her current skills gap?'
- 'Women in some patriarchal societies have become used to following their father's decisions. How can we make sure that women get decision-making practice?'
- 'Studies show that women have a significantly greater tendency to include various stakeholders and different viewpoints, ensuring the necessary consensus is in place to make sound decisions.'
- 'Women's decision-making style provides benefits for diversity, just like diversity adds value to other aspects of corporate life.'
- 'The pure fact of having diversity when making decisions is already leading to better decisions. Regardless of individuals not having strengths in this area: it is still beneficial to a company.'

Myth Ten

'Women Are Not Suited for Sales Positions'

Or 'For Production, or Creative Director, or . . .'

Uma Rudd Chia, who grew up in New Zealand, used to be the only female creative director globally at a leading advertising agency. 'When I hired a few women to my team, I was asked, 'Are you hiring them because they are women?' I answered, 'Yes, and they are just as good as men'. I believe that we need a balance of ideas, and we don't have that balance,' she said. She knows that we need the female perspective. 'The irony is that we are putting a filter of a man on advertising. But even for 60–70 per cent of men's products, women are decision-makers. We must stop looking at it purely from a male lens.'

Rudd Chia now runs a boutique creative agency with her business partner and shared stories of the challenges she faced as a female creative director—one of very few—that range from conforming with a masculine, even macho convention of what comprises good advertising, to sexual harassment and how to challenge and change the system. We know that advertising—advertisers and the target audiences alike—suffers from gender stereotyping,[156] and the energetic, confident, and multi-talented Rudd Chia seems on a mission to change the industry.

She knows the system reinforces itself. 'Male advertising bosses want rewards,' she said. As a former accounts director in the early 2000s at one of the leading advertising agencies myself, I know the focus on awards in the advertising industry. Winning awards are credentials that help us win more business in a cut-throat industry. 'The jury at award ceremonies are male, so they judge with a male lens. That means that they hire male creative directors because these will have a much better chance at winning awards,' Rudd Chia added. 'When I was a young creative, and I went to my first Cannes, it was all men.'

'It's getting better in recent years,' she stressed. Many award shows have male juries, and even the women on the jury have—like Rudd Chia said she had herself—viewed the world with a male lens. The Cannes Lions Festival, the world's most prestigious awards festival for advertising, at least, had a good gender balance in 2023: 57 per cent were men. Still not quite representing the women that make 80% of the purchasing decisions, according to Rudd Chia.

'To get great ideas, you really need diversity, and we need a diversity of ideas. You need diversity in terms of gender, culture, backgrounds, and much more,' Rudd Chia emphasized.

'I sat down in my boss's office—and he was the one who hired me, mind you. He said, "It's really hard for women because once she has a baby, you expect her to go home on time to her husband and make dinner and take care of her child. So, a lot of women drop off once they have a baby. So, there's no point in investing in them and hiring them." To his credit', she added, 'he hired me. But I, a woman, am sitting there. And he's telling me that there is no point in investing in or even hiring women.'

'The reason why there is a perception that women aren't fitting into this model or aren't great creative directors is because we are looking at it through a male lens of what a good idea looks like. They look at a male lens of what they think is going to sell.'

She appeared quite embarrassed when she added, 'I used to put on a male lens because I wanted to win awards,' which she did over the years en masse. 'Some of that work I am quite ashamed of now, to be honest. Now, I would not show it to my daughter. Everything changed for me when I had a daughter. I suddenly shifted from "someone's gotta change this" to "I'm not going to wait for 'someone' to change it. I'm going to change it because I'll be so embarrassed if my daughter walked into the room and heard this conversation."' Rudd Chia now actively supports gender equity in her industry and beyond.

Despite a high proportion of female staff at lower levels, the industry has been slow to tackle the 'boys' club' at senior levels, which has been hard for women to penetrate. And sexual harassment is 'normalized', as Rudd Chia and other anonymous voices tell me. Comments are often brushed away with 'oh, can't you take a joke?!'—a comment that we know today is a big red flag, indicating there might very well be a culture of sexual harassment. Yes, 'can't you take a joke' and 'you have no sense of humour' are very often indications of toxic culture—some form of harassment, whatever the underlying toxicity: sexual harassment, homophobia, racism . . . 'They would say to a colleague, "Hey, what are you wearing today, red underwear?" upon which I would yell through the room "That's sexual harassment!"' Rudd Chia said. Such a culture is not conducive to gender inclusion.

Rudd Chia excelled at her work. You have to, to be the only creative director in a leading advertising agency. Being successful in going at it alone—setting up her own boutique agency—further proves that she is great at what she does. Still, people around her doubt her judgement. 'I used to work for a skin product as the global creative director. I sat in meetings with old, male, western, white planners working out the strategy. When I wrote my stories, the men would say, "This is not the life they go through." I am a woman, and a man would tell *me*—an Asian mom, working, having to look after her kids—what the audience thinks? I'm at the same age of the audience, and I even speak their language!' she said, very offended.

'The worst thing on this campaign was when they suggested the tag line: "Women have the strength to be soft,"' Rudd Chia said, obviously outraged. I rolled my eyes upon hearing the tag line, which sounds like it's based on male wishful thinking rather than reality. She shared her sentiments of outrage from when she first heard it: 'You're telling me, you old British man who has never worn cream in your life why women wear a skin cream?! Every woman should have the right and find the strength to be who she is. Whether she wants to be soft or strong or whatever, don't put women in a box and say, "This is what a real woman should be like."'

'Why do you think women buy this cream?' she asked me rhetorically. 'Because it's cheap, it's affordable, and you just want to look good immediately. I simply don't have the time to get ready. Using this product is my shortcut. That's it. I need to look beautiful quickly or at least fix what I need to get fixed quickly.'

I can very much relate to wanting to look my best with minimal effort—in contrast to the suggested tag line by Rudd Chia's male colleagues. Don't tell me I need to be soft, please. And please, please don't tell me I'm not strong enough to be soft. It's unrelatable and even offensive to me.

Considering the influencing power of advertisements, we need more women in leadership positions in that industry. Rudd Chia has proven to the world that women are as great as men in key advertising roles, and we need to promote more women into senior positions quickly. Otherwise, the male perception of how women think and must behave will continue to see billions of advertisement dollars poured into it. It's also a matter of understanding your consumers. If they are women, make sure that you have women represented in the entire process, especially the decision-making process.

Are women unsuitable for sales?

'I joined sales at a point when women were not considered capable of doing sales,' Sharma told me. 'I joined sales with Pepsi at twenty-five years old as a fresh graduate from business school. I was ready for it despite the doubt in people around me that this was a suitable job for women,' she said. '"Do you understand what you are signing up for?" and "Do you understand the conditions?" I was asked by well-meaning relatives.'

'I was allocated to a warehouse as the only woman among 120 men—truck drivers, loaders, customer executives. I was the youngest and the only woman apart from the tea lady and an assistant. There was no female toilet, and they told me to go to the next-door restaurant and deal with it.'

'Truck drivers were at first sceptical, but they realized very quickly that I am professional, and I proved their fears of being high-maintenance unfounded. The most interesting experience were the dance bars—you know, bars where the customers are men, and the dancing ladies are the merchandise. The sales team were worried whether I would be comfortable to go to such an environment. I donned my Pepsi uniform and together with the team, made a dignified sales call. Not only did I manage to close the deal, I did so without any drama.' Sharma helped shatter the myth that women can't be in sales, and especially in the night entertainment industry.

'In my company, there is a real undertone that I have seen applied to many, many women, including myself. A female executive in the tech industry told me that "Women are given the strategy and planning roles, and men are given technical roles." Tech roles are the crown. You don't want to not have a technical role on your CV. I'm an engineer, but I wasn't even considered an expert in technology. My boss started giving me organizational tasks, such as setting up meetings. I was pigeon-holed. He commented once in a seemingly very surprised tone: "You're highly paid." Yes! I have a degree and I am good at what I do. I'm in senior management, so of course I went off and did something else.'

'First, they will treat you as very precious. Everyone wants to help you. But then, you become pigeon-holed, and you have to play "girly."' She was describing benevolent sexism, where we treat qualified women as if they're novices and keep them down through what appears like gallantry, but 'in fact it is because they don't know how to work with you as a woman, when, in fact, there should be no difference,' the IT executive said.

In a panel discussion that I attended, Murlidharan shared with the audience that in the recruiting industry, women predominantly recruit, and men do sales. She always liked sales and it is her career choice. 'I'm automatically seen as aggressive,' she said, sharing the public perception of assertive women automatically being seen as aggressive. And I know her—I have seen her in action. She is not aggressive. 'I don't push for sales. I build relations,' as she said. And there is evidence that women outperform men in sales, exactly because they tend to focus more on relationships.[157] Women listen 16 per cent more, which is essential in building trust, and that in turn is essential in closing sales. It results in women having 8 per cent higher quota attainment compared to men. And on average, 78 per cent of men achieve quota and 86 per cent of women do, as one study shows.[158]

One recruiting company asked her in a job interview whether she would be willing to wine and dine with clients, since that is required in a sales job. 'I didn't take the job, because I felt it was derogatory and demeaning just to ask me that question. Sadly, some recruiters also have the belief that some roles are more suitable for a specific gender,' she said. Recruiters have a massive impact on the make-up of a company, and with biases in the recruiting process, the narrative that women are not suitable for sales can be hard to shatter.

Challenges in traditionally male-dominated areas

Shipping and supply chain is a traditionally male-dominated industry. It's a challenge that UPS faces. Imagine your typical brown UPS truck—you will probably think of a male driver. Or handling shipments at the airport ramp—an image of a man probably comes to mind.

Despite being in a traditionally male-dominated industry, UPS have achieved gender balance in some of their functions. In addition, female representation in their management group—defined as those leading people—is about 44–45 per cent, which is significantly higher than most in the industry. Their global CEO is a woman, as is the president for Asia Pacific. The next level of leadership has good gender balance, too.

One area where they are still working on gender balance is operations. 'Think of the hardcore jobs,' Tanie Eio, who I worked with when she was leading HR in Asia Pacific, explained to me what operations entail in logistics. 'It's everyone who is involved in pick-up and delivery, from point to point—and everything in between.'

'Female representation in operations is around 25–27 per cent, which is a celebrated representation. We can still do more in that area,' she said. I don't even have to ask what drives her to improve the current balance. Being the diversity and inclusion champion she is, she automatically added, 'There is always room for improvement. It's an area where we have identified that we can do more. We believe in diversity and inclusion from selection, to training and promotions.' It's what sets companies apart in diversity and inclusions: Do those responsible truly believe it is important to have an inclusive culture, or are they checking of an item on a long list of priorities as a half-hearted attempt? Or are they even doing diversity and inclusion because they have been told to? Again, I recommend working on getting full commitment from leadership to both the moral and business case of inclusion, as UPS in APAC has.

Eio described staff in operations: 'We have female drivers, motorbike cyclists, workers at the airport ramp. Why is this even a topic of discussion when everyone should be eligible for any job?' She told me this almost dismissively while discussing the suitability of one gender for certain jobs. 'We all have a pair of eyes, which we don't discuss because it is natural and it is a given being human beings. Similarly, women should be given the option to choose and be welcomed to apply for any jobs of their choice. And I believe they can do a good job. You know the benefits of diversity, Mette, right?' she added.

Vescovi from Barilla also takes up the challenge as soon as he hears that it is difficult to find women in certain functions. Despite being told 'You can't find women in sales in Japan,' he hired a female sales director to the sales team there recently. And when he was told that 'China doesn't have women in supply chain,' he told the team to look harder.

When people speak their minds

Barilla is another company that supports my hypothesis that getting leadership to understand the benefits of inclusion and committing itself to it is essential for achieving results. They reached gender parity in leadership in Asia, Africa, and Australia in 2020—in Australia, the company has an all-women's leadership team as of 2022.

The company went through a painful process to reach these benchmarks and received the Catalyst Award 2021[159] for Diversity and Inclusion, a ceremony that I was honoured to attend.

Imagine Catholic Italy in 2013. Inclusion of the LGBTQ+ community is not on many people's mind. It's socially acceptable to mock people's sexual preferences.

Against this backdrop, the chairman of the company didn't realize that he was making a gaffe as the multinational leading pasta brand by saying 'I would never do a commercial with a homosexual family, not for lack of respect but because we don't agree with them. Ours is a classic family where the woman plays a fundamental role.'[160] At the time and place, many listening to the interview would not have recognized it as a gaffe and accepted it as a neutral fact.

The CEO, Claudio Colzani, had a background at Unilever where he even on the diversity committee. He was listening live to the interview, which otherwise was about more pleasant things such as pasta and knew he had an internal and external crisis that needed his immediate attention.

Within days, the chairman issued a video recorded apology, which did not hinder calls for a boycott by many consumers across North America and Europe. The immediate painful loss of market share was avoided, but Colzani worried about the longer-term effects of being perceived as an irrelevant and out-of-date brand.[161]

The company had already been focussing on healthy nutrition and environmental protection, and they felt that they were respecting individuals. What the incident shows is that we need to have conversations about diversity and inclusion in organizations, academia, government, and society as a whole to avoid what for you and I are obvious faux pas. With increased awareness and sensitivity, we can build inclusion with respect for all and avoid similar incidents. I'm not yet so ambitious to say 'eliminate'. That may need a generation or more of inclusion being part of society's DNA.

In my experience, similar stories play out very frequently. An off-the-cuff remark by a senior leader, sighing, 'Argh, we have to find a woman for this position,' can undo a dose of good work done by DEI (diversity, equity, and inclusion) officers and the grassroot DEI organizations, frequently called ERGs (to me the mysteriously and inappropriately labelled 'enterprise resource groups'—a fancy name that companies often call employee groups with the objective of promoting inclusion for particular groups of people, such as parents, women, LGBTQ+ people, etc.). Alternatively, take the Qatari Football World Cup ambassador, Khalid Salman, as an example. He damaged Qatar's image by calling homosexuality 'damage in the mind'[162] in an interview with German TV station ZDF. FIFA boss, Sepp Blatter, made another gaffe preceding the same event by telling gay people to 'refrain from any sexual activities' when in Qatar because sex between men is illegal there, for which he also had to apologize.[163]

Blatter apologized. I have not seen one by Salman.

Just like many of the very developed societies today would in the past have discriminated against, or simply dismissed women, people with different abilities, foreigners or migrants, those having different beliefs or political attitudes, and people from LGBTQ+ communities, there are plenty of places where it is still happening today.

We can hate and fight, or we can enter into a constructive dialogue, challenge their biases and beliefs, provide different perspectives, and include those with different beliefs.

It will be difficult. Let me give you an example from a recent dinner party. First, I need to explain benevolent sexism.

Benevolent sexism is when we treat women as weaker or less competent[6] as the female engineer quoted above reported

---

[6] For a great example of this phenomenon, see: Emma. 2020. 'Benevolent sexism: a feminist comic explains how it holds women back.' *The Guardian.* https://www.theguardian.com/books/2020/aug/13/benevolent-sexism-a-feminist-comic-explains-how-it-holds-women-back

what appears to be gallantry of men wanting to help can backfire and all of a sudden mean that you are classified as not capable of doing tough work. For instance, when a woman is told by a group of men, 'Oh, don't break your beautiful head over this. We will take care of it for you,' more than implying that she doesn't have the intelligence to handle it. Or a female tech engineer being told in a performance review, 'You're so nice and accepted by everyone. Your feminine touch is really great. It's so nice having you in the team,' instead of focussing on her accomplishments as an engineer. With a few performance reviews like that behind her, and a man's review having recorded 'cracked the bug in product A', 'persuaded the customer to collaborate on the development of product B, leading to a 10 per cent increases in sales', who do you think is more likely to get that next promotion? Men in general do get more specific and action-based feedback than women, and this is one of the many obstacles in the path for women's promotion.

Benevolent sexism extends to romantic encounters. Holding the door for the woman. Vacating a seat on public transport for a woman (yes, schools in the Netherlands taught this to kids when I was in primary school there in the seventies. Vacate your seat for women and the elderly.) Paying the bill on the first date.

I'm all for holding the door for others. If it is gender related, though, we're implying that women are weak. I was very grateful when I got a seat while returning from Nagoya to Tokyo on a trip in a very full Shinkansen and being seven or so months pregnant. Getting up for those who truly need it is not just fully acceptable, it is basic human kindness that I hope we all have in abundance. Getting up simply because someone is female is implying she is weaker.

Now at the recent dinner with some female friends, some of them insisted that a man must pay on the first date. 'Why?' I inquired. 'Because you need to know that they are not stingy. I want someone who is generous,' was the answer. We are talking about emancipated, well-earning women. And how will the woman show generosity on her first date?

There are two issues here. First, we know the effects of the reciprocity bias. We are much more open to return a favour. That favour can very well be laughing at his jokes that are not really that humorous, not contradicting an opinion, or even sexual favours. We know reciprocity bias is an impulse that is very ingrained in humans, and why would we let ourselves fall for this?

Second, we are setting ourselves up for who plays what role in the relationship. The women in question were, in some cases, even better able to afford the dining bill, but they felt very strongly about adhering to the tradition that the man must pay the bill on the first date. Again, if it weren't about gender—and I personally enjoy paying if we are at a restaurant that I could afford much better than whomever I go out dining with, regardless of gender— it is okay that one person pays. If it has to be the woman, it's benevolent sexism, implying that the woman, the 'weaker gender', cannot pay.

One of the women at the dinner party was sharing outraging stories about her dating, making the other women feel very offended by men's behaviour. I tried to put some responsibility on her without much luck. It seems like she is attracting men who do not treat her with respect.

It starts with respecting yourself. Either gender can show generosity. Either gender can show kindness. But if you are falling into the role of being the weaker person who must be provided for and protected, who does not speak up for herself, and who laughs at comments that are just not funny, you are helping maintain gender stereotypes. You are deciding what the gender roles will be in the relationship from that first date onward.

This is difficult to accept because it is one of the many stories that we have bought into: Men are supposed to be our providers. And this is a narrative that can be the easiest to shatter of all. To make a difference, all we need to do is to wave that credit card at the waiter.

We're at a moment in time where catalytic change is possible

We're still seeing media articles and posts about 'the first Black person in . . .' or 'the first Asian woman in . . .' Sometimes the social media posts are followed by, 'We have these posts so often. Women are everywhere. Stop posting these!' The very truth is that these will come to an end when it is not the first woman, or minority representative any more. When it is not 'news', it won't be posted as such.

I am very convinced that this will change soon. Although my parents would probably not have expected that their daughters would still face inclusion challenges since they invested in our education, the speed of change has accelerated. Although it will take 257 years to close the global gender pay gap at the current speed,[164] a number that increased during COVID-19, I do see the awareness increasing, as well as the sense of urgency. And true commitment, as mentioned above, can make a true difference. The company that I left a decade ago because I felt dismissed and saw no career prospects despite a lot of talk, is now promoting more women, and on track to have 30 per cent women in leadership roles by 2023.

I am in general an optimistic person, and I am certain that inclusion will have further momentum if those of us who strongly believe in it will continuously be committed to advocate, activate, champion, stand up for, and drive inclusion. I'm convinced that we are at a moment in history where catalytic change is possible.

In teaching—a male profession until the beginning of the nineteenth century—women meanwhile make up 71 per cent of primary school teachers in East and Southeast Asia and 57 per cent of secondary school teachers. The number of women medical doctors have increased in all OECD countries, and in the Nordic countries, there's either gender parity or women doctors now outnumber their male colleagues.[165]

This shows that it's our culture that tells us what women can and cannot do and that it is a worldwide trend.

In July 2018, women were finally allowed to be behind the steering wheel in Saudi Arabia, and today, women are more and more encouraged to enter the workforce. For most of you readers, I'm sure that this appears an archaic thought. However, we can take examples that are very recent that show that development comes in steps. Even up to the 1970s, the BBC claimed that women's voices weren't considered suitable for news reading: The head of radio LE (Light Entertainment), thought, 'The pitch of the female voice makes it inappropriate for the opening and closing announcements of his programmes.' The head of TV presentation was equally insulting of female voices: 'A woman's voice attracts too much attention. Announcing . . . represents the supreme authority and a man's voice is suited to all occasions by tradition' and there is 'the problem of women having unsuitable "Lah-di-dah" voices.'[166]

Even in 2017, when I founded KeyNote Women Speakers, a community and directory of women speakers, I was told by a male friend that he 'prefers to listen to men speak'. He admitted that he perceives men as the experts. It was an honest and spontaneous answer, which I appreciate. He doesn't show any disrespect to women otherwise. It simply shows that our biases prevail.

Without honest, open, non-judgemental conversations, while engaging in curious, constructive dialogue that assumes positive intent, we will not advance inclusion.

Meanwhile, successful female doctors, lawyers, politicians, news readers, salespeople, and creative directors have proven that these beliefs are exactly that: Unconscious biases that are not founded in truth.

As more and more countries experience increased numbers of women entering the workforce, we are discovering that gender is not the best indicator of whether someone is good at a certain role. The variation within one gender is much larger than between the two main genders: women and men.

It's not easy to break these beliefs. Often, we will be unsuccessful, despite having the facts on our sides, as I have encountered time and time again. It can be discouraging. I'm driven by a commitment to fairness and have accepted that many will find the simple fact that I address inequalities and inequities annoying. I recently experienced this while addressing male toxicity at an International Women's Day event. The (male) managing director addressed me during the break, mentioning that it was wrong for me to mention toxic masculinity on International Women's Day. It was a five-minute discussion during a four-hour session. He was not convinced that this could be related, because he has a deeply held belief that the topic itself is damaging. I found it very relevant, as I put in in the context that a culture of toxic masculinity can make it difficult for women to be accepted at an equal level, and it was in no way the focus of the event. And even if it was irrelevant—if I spoke about coffee production in Brazil for five minutes during a four-hour financial presentation, I would probably not have the MD walk up to me and complain. It shows how emotions run high, and how difficult it is for us to have constructive conversations.

Shattering the myth that women are not suitable for certain positions

When confronted with the argument that women are not suitable for a position, you can challenge the myth by saying:

- 'Vast evidence across a wide range of industries shows that women can be very successful in industries they weren't considered suitable for in the past. This stretches back to when women weren't considered suitable politicians, medical doctors, or even teachers—professions that today see an increasing number of women. In the case of teachers, women now frequently outnumber men.'

- 'It's our perception and our culture that have prescribed women unsuitable for this position. Just look at wartimes. Women had to do the jobs that men did because they went off to fight. And they did those jobs well.'

- 'There may be statistical differences between the competencies and characteristics of women and men. However, this doesn't necessarily mean that a single gender is unsuited for one particular role. There's a much larger variation and distribution of skills within each gender rather than between them.'

- Often, women are held back by a lack of facilities, such as no female toilet access. In that case, let's change that: 'How about we solve it by installing more toilets (or the other facilities such as nursing rooms, childcare facilities, increasing safety, etc.) which makes the environment suitable for women and helps us create a truly inclusive culture?'

- 'What can we do to make this woke environment accessible to women?'

- 'What can we do to make women better at the skills needed for this position?'

- 'What are the reasons that you see this position as unsuitable for women?'

- 'What do you think women could bring to the function that could be strengthened in them?'

Section II

Skills for Speaking Up and Dispelling the Myths Effectively

When you begin to use the arguments provided throughout this book to shatter the narratives and dispel the myths that hold women back at work, certain communication skills may be helpful. My hope is that the arguments and skills help you get your points across in a way that allow you to truly be heard rather than being dismissed. It takes courage to challenge the status quo, and the better our communication skills, the more confident we feel and the more relaxed we can be in our discussions.

I have attempted to be factual rather than provoking arguments in the book. But there's still no guarantee that some people won't feel provoked by them. Sometimes, the truth can be embarrassing or threatening to people. And sometimes, your counterpart may be unable to take a different perspective. I also realize that different workplaces have different levels of 'psychological safety' or cultures based on interpersonal trust and mutual respect.[167] So, in this section, I'll provide guidance on having constructive conversations in a variety of settings and cultures.

It helps to practise what you want to say on your own and try out your points in a friendlier environment at first. Then, it might be easier to structure your counterarguments effectively. I always practise my arguments before participating in a panel discussion. I define the 'sound bites' I want to include as easy-to-remember short statements, saying them out loud to myself until I know them well. I'm getting better at it with each experience. For those of us who are not born with eloquence, practice is key.

Patience

As any change manager will tell us, humans tend to resist change. In addition, we may find ourselves challenging people who have more power than us in their position. They may be accustomed to having the upper hand. It's only human for people to feel reluctant to fully share such privileges with others. Plus, the narratives and beliefs that I describe in this book can be deeply held, widespread, and tenacious.

For instance, some women may *say* and *believe* they don't want a career. When we ask for their reasons, they might say it's too stressful in addition to their other responsibilities, or that they can't be bothered with the politics, or don't want to be in a position where they fear they will be poorly treated. I've provided several examples of highly qualified women who resigned from their jobs in large multinational companies because they felt unfairly treated and didn't want to play the game any longer. And I find it highly likely that some of these women would feel differently if it were easier for them to have a thriving career.

In one of my workshops, a woman was convinced she didn't want a higher leadership position or a big career. I saw plenty of talent in her, and I asked, 'What would your boldest career plan be if you were a man?' In a split second, her imagination fired up. Ever since that spontaneous challenge I gave this female middle management leader, I have used it in Women in Leadership workshops when designing their audacious career goals. And it works every time. A woman will pick up her pen, think big, and define a bold career plan when pretending to be a man.

This shows that many women would want a career if the corporate world would make it easier for them to nurture one, but instead, even some women themselves are convinced they aren't interested in advancements, which just feeds into the myth.

In other words, our assumptions run deep, and challenging them may take patience on everyone's part.

So, don't expect all of your conversations to be easy. Some may very well be, while others may be difficult. My hope is that this book will make it easier for you to speak up and change these persistent narratives that hold women back. If we all do what we can, we have the capacity to improve the professional world for women across the globe.

Skill One

Choose Your Audience Wisely

Strategizing about the audience to target becomes easier when we divide our audience into three parts, say 20 per cent–60 per cent–20 per cent.[168] These numbers represent two equally sized groups of people with a positive and negative opinion, plus a large middle 60 per cent (stressing that these are just 'typical' numbers). We often focus on the 20 per cent negatives—those who disagree with us—and we end up being locked into the 20-60-20 ratio rather than changing it.

This doesn't take into account that many of the people who strongly disagree with us are difficult to persuade no matter what we say or do. It's partly a mindset. These may be people who tend to always see the glass as half empty. We could pour a lot of energy into their half-empty glasses, trying to be persuasive without ever filling them up. The return on energy investment is low.

Or we might find that our deeply held values and beliefs differ so significantly from the other person that finding common ground will provide an equally low return.

Sometimes, it's healthier to walk away than stay in a toxic situation. Whitney Wolfe Herd, CEO and founder of the dating app Bumble, tells a great story about finding your right audience and choosing to walk away. In February 2021, she became the world's youngest female CEO to take her company public in the US,[169] as well as the world's youngest self-made billionaire. But it hadn't always been easy for her. She was one of the co-founders of the world's largest dating app, Tinder, where her ideas were seemingly ignored. She alleges that she experienced harassment and was stripped of her co-founder title. As a result, she sued Tinder and settled out of court. Then, she continued her quest to create a women's-empowerment-centric dating app and eventually succeeded in finding the right funding to launch Bumble.[170] Whitney's story is a perfect example of how great ideas shared with the wrong people may be dismissed or stifled, but finding the right circle of supporters for our idea can take it to the next level.

Since it's harder to shift those who have already made up their minds, our best bet is to approach those who are flexible about their positions. Therefore, it's much more effective to focus on the 60 per cent who may be on the fence. This is no different to a vote in the US. Political candidates have a hard time convincing the core of the other party to vote for them, so they focus on 'swing voters'.

We are ignoring the 20 per cent that are on our side. Unless you need to rally more support, you're not getting too much out of preaching to the choir.

Focus on those you can persuade: the 60 per cent

The best way to win our case is to read the room and evaluate whether it will serve our purpose to take a stand.

We may, of course, first choose to focus on the 20 per cent positives. For instance, these could be potential allies and advocates for our cause. When we're in the minority or have lower influencing power than others in the room, we can make more progress by teaming up with others and increasing our collective bargaining power. Together, we can make a difference when engaging the middle 60 per cent. By appealing to the middle 60 and their sense of fairness, our movement may gain momentum. Then, when we've gained the hearts and minds of the majority, it's easy to become a self-reinforcing process.

Some in the audience will receive our arguments as new. Like with all new things, it may take time for them to adjust. Therefore, our communication skills are key to engaging the 60 per cent. It's a balancing act to be clear, informative, and interesting.

In our numerous webinars on bias and inclusion, we have found that we get the best results in persuasion on inclusion when we focus on values. When a leadership team has first discussed *why* they would like to have an inclusive culture based on a values discussion, it is difficult for them to back out again. Most people want to be at least fair and respectful, and value others for their contribution. Most people cringe when we put up the definition of biases, which include words such as 'closed-minded', 'prejudicial', and 'unfair'. Who wants to be guilty of this? Nobody we have come across yet.

Definition of Bias[171]

'Bias is a disproportionate weight in favour of or against an idea or thing, usually in a way that is closed-minded, prejudicial, or unfair. Biases can be innate or learned. People may develop biases for or against an individual, a group, or a belief.'

Exercise

Which battles to choose?

Is there a narrative that is holding you back or a situation that really irks you?

Consider:

- Who could be your ally to support you and have your back?
- Who are influencers, who can further influence important stakeholders?
- Are there people who are on the fence or open to a change and who are easier to persuade to create a critical mass on your side of the argument?
- What arguments and what communication style is most suitable for these people?

Also, consider:

- What is their point of view? What is true about it? What are their interests?
- And, if the other person is simply against you for the sake of being argumentative or stubborn, that's an audience to probably walk away from.

Skill Two

Separating Impact from Intent

How often have you heard someone say something that shocked you, and after you reacted, they said, 'That's not what I meant!' You may even have responded, 'But that's what you said!' It's so easy to be unclear or misunderstood.

Often, when we speak, we focus primarily on our *intent;* on the message we want to get across.

On the other hand, when we listen, we tend to focus on the *impact* the other person's words have on us.

Regardless of whether we're speaking or listening, we could consider both the intent and the impact. As a speaker, it's a good idea to ask ourselves: What's our intent? How might it impact the listener? What's their perspective?

As listerners, it's a good idea to ask ourselves: What's the speaker's intent? What's their perspective? Would it be helpful to let them know how their words impact us?

In the two-way street of effective communication, we need to equally have a two-way street of seeking to understand impact *and* intent.

Different communication styles

As we evaluate intent and impact, it's important to take different communication styles into account. Some people are concise, direct, and brief in their communication, while others prefer flowery, indirect, and more lengthy descriptions. When we're from a homogenous background with the other person, speaking the same language, communication is easier. We've been taught the same style, and our upbringing may even result in 'insider lingo'.

But even in our own environment, such as our family, misunderstandings are very common. Between men and women, for example, which gender do you think is more likely to say, 'The dishes aren't done yet,' rather than 'Would you please do the dishes?'

Women are more likely to be indirect in their requests, and the desired impact is less likely to be achieved. A person with a preference for more direct communication may even take 'the dishes aren't done yet' as a statement rather than a request to solve the issue.

As I mentioned in the introduction, when our body language, tonality, facial expressions, and tone of voice are out of sync with our words, we believe facial expressions the most, then tonality, and finally words. With any of these being incongruent, we inadvertently create an open invitation for miscommunication.

We also sometimes find we use language differently from others. True story: A woman overheard her teenagers using the phrase 'Netflix and chill' and assumed it meant 'watching Netflix and taking it easy'. After using the phrase in a social media post that brought amused responses, she checked the definition: 'sexual activity, either as part of a romantic partnership, as casual sex, or as a groupie invitation'.

Even when speaking to someone from your culture, in the same language, miscommunication is abundant. And since others may have very different perspectives on the arguments in this book, our communication is more effective when . . .

- We assume the other person has positive intent, while acknowledging that they have different experiences and opinions. In other words, we may know they have a different viewpoint or stance, but we assume they don't intend to offend, hurt, or hold us down.
- We stop giving ourselves automatic and unfiltered credit for good intent when the impact on the other party is negative.
- We work hard to minimize the negative impact of our words by considering their impact.

Simply put, considering both impact and intent, as well as different communication styles and language use, helps us reduce communication clashes.

Exercise

Look at each of the following sentences:

- It's easier to accept that the business world is dominated by men.
- Women are made to be the caretakers.
- Male leaders have no idea how to be inclusive.

Consider responding to each of these in the following ways:

- Imagine you're hearing the sentence. What do you expect is the speaker's intent? Stretch yourself by finding three different possible intentions.

- Now, imagine you're the speaker of the sentence. How might it impact the listener? Again, see if you can identify three different ways it might affect an audience.
- If a conversation is on the verge of escalating into an argument because of the difference in impact and intent of the speaker and listener, how would you propose managing the situation?

Skill Three

Empathy and Compassion

Have you ever noticed that saying 'calm down' to an angry person is like throwing petrol on a fire? It has the opposite effect of what we intend. When we don't take the other party's emotional frame of mind into account, a conversation can quickly escalate. If we're discussing something at a rational level, but our listener is in an emotional state, our words are likely to be ineffective.

I'm from a family where we didn't shout at each other. I can't recall my parents ever shouting at my sister and me. My husband has quite a different upbringing with a father who would be strict as well as raise his voice. We do as we are taught, so one day, when our then still-toddler son was screaming in his room, my husband shouted: 'Stop screaming!'

I started laughing, which is when my husband saw the irony in it. He's worked very hard on keeping his calm in general, and today, decades later, is probably better at managing his emotions than I am.

The reason it's difficult to listen when we're upset is that the emotional centre of the brain (the amygdala) has hijacked and deactivated our highly advanced, thinking brain (the frontal lobe). We know that when exposed to danger, the amygdala takes over, and we have three main options: fight, flight, or freeze.[172] It's similar with emotions, which is why saying 'calm down' doesn't work: Our brain is impaired. When someone is stuck in their emotional brain, they can't connect with rational arguments.

Consider an upset child who is crying loudly. You've probably seen parents tell the kid to stop crying. If anything, the situation gets worse, perhaps with the parent starting to scream. What happens, instead, when the parent takes the child in their arms, asking why they're upset and wiping away the tears? Which approach do you think is more effective?

Adults are not that much different to the crying toddler, although I'm certainly not advocating that we take a colleague into our arms in a business situation. But when we're speaking to someone who is upset, it's more effective to first address the emotions by showing empathy. When our emotions are addressed, we feel heard, seen, and valued—a great remedy against emotional upheaval. Then, once the person's emotions have calmed down, we can move to rational arguments.

When we address emotions first, we increase our likelihood of a constructive conversation. When we are emotional, we humans need emotional relatedness in order to have a constructive conversation. At the least, we want to be heard, seen, and preferably even understood and valued.

How to address emotions and show empathy

The first step is recognizing that emotions are at play. Some expressions of emotions are obvious, such as raising your voice, even shouting. How do you gauge another person's reaction when the signs are more subtle than screaming and slamming a fist on the table, though? Think about your own reactions. When you're upset, does your heart rate speed up? Do you take shallow breaths? Do you freeze or feel like walking away when faced with a highly stressful situation? And do you easily read and recognize these cues in other people?

Bear in mind, however, that we all respond to stress and conflict differently, so other people's reactions may not be the same as yours. When we're having a challenging conversation, it can be helpful to pay attention to the small and big changes in the composure of the other person in order to assess their emotional reaction to the best of our ability. Then, we can better discern the impact of our intent.

Once we assess the other person's emotions, we can acknowledge those feelings with empathy and compassion. Note that empathy and sympathy differ. 'Sympathy involves understanding from your own perspective. Empathy involves putting yourself in the other person's shoes and understanding why they may have these particular feelings.'[173] Compassion is going a step further and showing a willingness to alleviate the person's suffering[174] without trying to merely fix it, of course. Here, we will focus on showing empathy.

For example, if someone feels threatened by the additional competition when women are promoted, it's a good idea to address that. Take a colleague who complains, 'Men don't get fair consideration for promotions in the company any longer because the focus is only on women.' Consider first responding, 'I understand that it is frustrating for you to see women promoted when you feel equally qualified for the position.' Then, wait for their reaction, using the power of the pause to see whether the empathy is working. If you addressed the right emotion, there will likely be a positive reaction.

I know it may be difficult to empathize with someone if we find their opinion abhorrent, but whether or not we agree with them, we can certainly look at the situation from their perspective.

This helps us better understand how to collaborate with them successfully and reach common ground.

Be warned: It doesn't always work. As with all communication advice, there's no guarantee for success. But I will guarantee that on average, you will be better off when getting better at the skills that we briefly mention here.

Exercise

The exercises on impact and intent helps you empathize with others. Practising empathy improves your ability to communicate and collaborate.

Let's look at some responses you might have to another people's feelings. You decide which are empathy, sympathy, or a lack of both:

Statement

Is it empathy, sympathy, or neither?

I can see you are upset.	
You're so unlucky.	
I have no idea what you're going through.	
That must be so devastating.	
I can see that this is very difficult for you.	
You should just ignore them.	
You must be frustrated.	
Is it really that bad?	
What are you up to now?	

I've experienced exactly the same.	
I'm so sorry for your loss.	
Best to get back on your feet immediately.	
What happened?	
Oh, no!	
How could things get this bad?	
Why didn't you tell me earlier?	
Try and look at the bright side.	
Poor thing!	

Of course, all of these statements are out of context, which means there's no absolute right or wrong answer. To help you go one step further in understanding empathy, look at each statement again, think whether you have said these words and ask yourself:

- Was the statement about them or about you? Did you ask so that you would understand because you were curious or because it would help them? If it's mostly about you and to rationally understand, you may have showed sympathy, or neither sympathy nor empathy.
- Did you consider their perspective (empathy) or mostly interpret their situation based on your own experiences (sympathy)?
- Were you bringing yourself to the person in the situation and even feelings? (Which is sympathy if you were seeing it from your perspective, and empathy if you were putting yourself in their shoes)
- Was the statement judgemental? Perhaps you showed pity more than anything else?

- Consider whether you're meeting the other person on an emotional level or whether you're still in your head, which means it's neither empathy nor sympathy.
- Were you offering help? In that case, you were probably rational about it rather than addressing emotions by listening and understanding what they are going through.

Skill Four

Managing Your Own Emotions

We're all triggered to some extent when we feel that our core values and beliefs are questioned. It takes an extremely emotionally balanced person to avoid reacting when these are triggered. I'm definitely still working on managing my emotions, which is a continuous process for most of us.

I can only take so much before I risk losing my temper, like when someone says that women aren't made for leadership. Or when I'm interrupted more frequently than the men in the room. Or when I'm being 'mansplained' to—which is when a man assumes women are lesser informed or intelligent beings and explains things in a condescending or patronizing way. In these situations, my core values of mutual respect and fairness are the triggers.

Of course, there's nothing wrong with emotions. They include passion, enthusiasm, and compassion. But emotions can also hinder progress in a discussion, as I recently experienced. The topic was 'angry women', and I got triggered because I was repeatedly interrupted and felt unheard. I was then immediately labelled as one of those 'angry women', and the discussion went sour, as you can imagine.

How to calm down when you are triggered

I learned the technique of 'labelling' from a friend almost a decade ago, and I'm still fascinated by how effective it is. I regularly remind myself to use it when I feel negative feelings boiling up.

Labelling is a trick that helps you move your emotions out of the core, primitive part of your brain (the amygdala) and into the frontal lobe. We do this by analysing our emotions rationally to find out what is going on. Saying 'I am stressed because of the amount of work,' helps you become more emotionally aware, especially when you put more granular labels on it, such as 'I feel overwhelmed with the amount of work I commit myself to do.'

When we combine it with the Seven Whys technique, or at least ask yourself great questions until you get to the cause of your emotional upheaval, it further deactivates the amygdala and activates the frontal lobe instead. The rationalization about what is going on calms emotions.

Ask, for instance, 'Why am I emotionally affected?' We continue to ask ourselves about the root cause until we've calmed down. If we ask the right, non-judgemental questions, we arrive at the core reason for our emotional reaction, which usually has to do with our personal values and strongly held beliefs.

Another way to label our emotions and calm down is to change our inner voice from 'I'm angry' to 'I'm experiencing the feeling of anger.' This forces us to think rationally about our emotions, rather than become consumed by them. We can use this with judgements as well by changing the thought, 'He's so incompetent,' to 'I'm having the thought that he's incompetent.' It works wonders.

Here are some additional preferred tips for managing emotions:

- Slow, deep breathing. Open up under-used parts of your lungs. Make sure you exhale too. Breathing out also relaxes you.

- Stepping out for a moment, doing something completely different. Grabbing a glass of water. Going to the loo.
- Counting backwards from 100 to one. By engaging our rational brain in this way, we move our thoughts out of the central part of our brain. It's so calming that I also often use this technique to fall asleep.
- Sleeping on it. Emotions sometimes subside overnight, because during sleep, our brain compartmentalizes information, filing it away.
- Discussing it with someone who will listen and understand our perspective as well as challenge us to see their perspective. In this way, we gain clarity, which gives us the insight to respond with better, well-considered arguments.
- Asking ourselves if this will matter in one, three, or five years. Considering time and the bigger picture can be an effective way to adjust our perspective.

Exercise

Why don't you practise the labelling technique and ask seven questions to get to the bottom of what is going on emotionally right now? It only takes a minute. Think of the last situation when you felt upset, perhaps during an interaction with one of your loved ones. Start by rephrasing it to 'I experienced the feeling of . . .' or 'I had the thought that . . .'

Next, ask yourself questions like these:

- What was the emotion you experienced?
- Can you think of a more detailed way of describing the emotion?
- Why did this happen? Most of us 'blame' someone else first. But go deeper and ask if the harm you felt was

truly their intention. What do you think was their actual intention?

- Now, try to understand why you were so affected by the situation. Focus on what happened inside of you to bring about the emotion, not what someone else did.

Keep digging deeper and asking 'why' until you have the clarity you need.

Here's an example that isn't related to gender equality of how I used this technique. We have a clear division of responsibilities in our household—the men do the dishes and the women do the laundry. One day, I came home after a long day of work and had exactly half an hour to get food and drinks ready for a dozen friends who were coming over. I was carrying the groceries, ready to quickly prepare everything when I saw that the kitchen was a mess—the worst it had ever been. There wasn't even space to put the groceries on the counter, let alone to prepare the food.

The emotional centre in my brain was immediately activated. My first thought was, 'That's so disrespectful to leave me with this huge mess when I have a tight schedule!' Then, I remembered labelling and the Seven Whys techniques.

I asked myself, 'What are my emotions?'

The answer was 'Disrespected!'

'Does my husband disrespect me?' (Digging deeper; keeping the discussion with yourself honest and real.)

'No, in fact, he highly respects my professional achievements.'

'So, what happened?'

'He probably lost track of time and had to rush out for a meeting.'

'And is it a big deal?'

'No, the people coming over are friends. They won't mind helping me get the wine, cheese, bread, veggie sticks, and dips prepared.'

The emotions disappeared. Unfortunately, I had already sent an angry text message to my husband. Next time, I decided to practise managing my emotions before I hit the 'send' button!

Skill Five

Asking Questions Rather Than Making Statements

In most of the arguments I've mentioned in this book, I have included the questions technique. Not only does it evoke higher levels of empathy and a much friendlier exchange of thoughts, but open-ended, neutral questions involve the other person too. This means that we show respect for their intellectual and emotional capabilities.

Most of us don't ask enough questions, and there are many reasons for that. In a Harvard Business School publication, the authors suggested it's because 'most people just don't understand how beneficial good questioning can be'.[175]

The first benefit is that open-ended, neutral, and non-judgemental questions provide us with more information about the other person's opinions, values, beliefs, drivers, wants, needs, and even fears. (Remember what we learned in primary school? Open-ended questions are those that don't elicit a single-word response like 'yes', 'no', 'tomorrow', or 'blue'.) As a result, we often learn about new and surprising perspectives. If we're curious and truly open to understanding, we may even learn that the other person has a valid point.

Of course, this means we may have to let go of the need to be 'right'.

The second benefit is building trusted relationships. People like us more when we ask questions with curiosity. It's a good basis for constructive conversations about gender equity.

A third benefit of asking questions is used by reporters: Questions help us maintain the upper hand in the conversation.

One disclaimer, this technique won't work for long if (1) we aren't genuinely curious about the answer, (2) we're signalling that we aren't listening and don't truly care, (3) we aren't open to accept that the other person could be right, (4) we aren't open to being wrong, or (5) we show that we're using the technique simply to deal a blow later.

The questioning technique in action

I once worked with a person who had the questioning technique all figured out . . . or so she thought. She would ask three, four, or five questions before she would start yelling accusations. I have since concluded that she was fishing for evidence that the other person was wrong and just waiting to attack. Needless to say, people around her learned to keep their guard up when she started asking questions with that phony, caring smile on her face.

On the other hand, when we ask not just one, but several open-ended, neutral, non-judgemental questions and genuinely listen, people feel heard and respected. Questions are a powerful way to open someone's mind about the topic.

Take, for instance, the narrative, 'Women prioritize children and family over career.' To combat it, we could ask: 'What are the most important factors in getting mothers to continue their careers after they have children?' Or, 'What can we do to make working in our company attractive to mothers?'

Of course, we'll sometimes encounter strongly opinionated conservatives who will answer, 'Nothing! Women are only interested in children.' But even so, questioning makes it more likely that the person will start thinking about the root cause and solutions rather than dwelling on a narrative that isn't supported by the evidence.

Exercise

Try changing the sentences below.

Let's start with a general business example. Your peer or business partner (bottom line: someone equal to you) made a poor investment decision in your view.

You could state:

- 'Your decision to invest in this business is a big failure.'

Now, try rewriting it. How can you make this into a question?

_____

_____

_____

Here is one more general example, choose the details of your scenario. You could state:

- 'The pricing of this product is too low.'

How can you turn this into a question?

_____

_____

_____

You could state:

- 'Management doesn't like this.'

How can you change this into a question?

_____

_____

_____

Now, try a few that are highly relevant to this book.
You could state:

- 'You're neglecting all the women in your department.'

How can you make this a question to get a constructive conversation going?

_____

_____

_____

You could state:

- 'Women aren't too emotional to be leaders!'

How can you make this a question to get a constructive conversation going?

_____

_____

_____

Skill Six

Ensuring Your Questions Are Neutral

You've just practised open-ended questioning. What about the open-ended but non-neutral and very judgemental question, 'Why do you fear women so much?' This question makes assumptions about the other person and is accusatory. Unless the person has just admitted to fearing women, it's unlikely to lead to a constructive conversation. We'd get rather defensive when confronted with such an accusation. Quite a few people have been brought up to be brave, and if they're accused of being fearful, they're likely to enter an emotional state without the ability to listen to rational arguments. Remember that we need to avoid activating the emotional part of the other person's brain.

Let's take another question that would probably result in a confrontation, compared to one that would more likely result in a constructive exchange. Imagine the following question asked in a sharp tone of voice: 'Why don't you promote more women into leadership positions?'

What do you think the other person would feel when asked this question? If asked in a judgemental tone, the other person would probably hear it as an accusation rather than a neutral query. And how do we react to accusations? Do we reflect on the idea? Usually not. The question would probably lead to a verbal boxing match in which one person tries to deal a blow, while the other person defends, prepared to return another blow.

What's your communication approach—boxing or dancing?

Dancing is when we aim to create something fun, inspirational, and beautiful together. It's when we feel, observe, and react to the other person's signs and further build on this knowledge. With a 'dancing' mindset, the previous question could be changed to: 'What do you think about gender balance in leadership?'

The first conversation ('Why do you fear women so much?') would almost certainly quickly lead to a stalemate with nobody changing positions, while the last question ('What do you think about gender balance in leadership?') would have a better chance of moving the complex issue of gender inequality forward.

Responses to narratives that can help advance the gender equality cause include:

- 'What makes you think so?'
- 'What are your experiences in this area?'
- 'What are the pros and cons?'

What makes a question a powerful one that advances the discussion? The questions used by executive coaches, for example, are helpful, such as 'Tell me more,' and 'What else?' Through questions like these, we can potentially steer the conversation away from an argument.

Remember, however, that non-verbal language plays a big role. It's easy to say these sentences with an accusatory tone of voice. We can make it sound as if we've added 'on earth', to the statement, making it sound like, 'What *on earth* makes you think so?!' If we're just slightly emotionally triggered during the discussion, our non-verbal language is likely to give this away.

The importance of the Ws

You might have noticed that my suggested questions mainly started with 'what'. This is no coincidence. 'Why' may start open questions, but they can be more problematic. 'Why' is often perceived as an attack.

For instance: 'What makes you think so?' versus 'Why do you think so?'

Can you hear that the 'why' version of the question is at least slightly more accusatory? This is especially true if it's the first question we pose someone in a loaded conversation. In a follow-up question, it might be heard more as genuine interest in understanding underlying motivations and beliefs.

The other main questioning words—'when', 'who', 'where', and 'which'—are typically used for clarification purposes. In fact, if we use them too frequently in sequence, the person may feel that they're being interrogated. Imagine being asked questions like this:

A: 'Where are you from?'
B: 'Denmark'
A: 'How long are you in Singapore?'
B: 'Fourteen years'
A: 'You like the food here?'
B: 'Yes'
A: 'Can you eat spicy things?'
B: 'Yes'
A: 'Have you gotten used to the weather?'
B: 'Yes'

A: 'Is your family with you?'

B: 'Yes'

A: 'Are you a teacher here?'

B: 'No'

A: 'What does your husband do?'

Having lived outside my country of birth for over forty-five years, I've been questioned this way countless times. At the receiving end, I do feel uncomfortable having to answer the questions. The questions are all closed with one possible correct answer.

Questioning can quickly feel like interrogation and put people on the defensive, which takes us back to boxing. 'What' is usually a better strategy, although I purposely added a 'what' question to the above conversation to show that asking 'what' isn't fool proof strategy. If we instead ask, 'What brings you to Singapore?' the conversation is more likely to get interesting. We may discover things we would never have thought to ask about. Neither of the conversationalists feels intimidated and both are much more likely to enjoy it when asked for their stories, rather than being put in boxes. Asking open-ended, non-judgemental questions gives the impression that you are interested in the person, rather than responding to your own need for establishing how the two of us differ.

Exercise

Review your answers from the previous skills exercise. Were they non-judgemental? If not, this skills discussion should help you. Review the same statements and questions here.

You could state:

- 'Your decision to invest in this business is a big failure.'

Or you could ask a question:

- 'Why did you invest in this loss-making business?'

Now, review and rewrite it, if needed, into a less leading and more open-ended question. Try to start with 'what':

_____

_____

_____

You could state:

- 'The pricing of this product is too low.'

Or you could ask a question:

- 'Why did you price the product so low?'

How can you make this question less leading, and more open-ended?

_____

_____

_____

You could state:

- 'Management doesn't like this.'

How can you change this into a less leading, and open-ended question?

_____

_____

_____

Now, try a few that are highly relevant to this book.
You could state:

- 'You're neglecting all the women in your department.'

How can you make this a non-leading and open-ended
question to get a constructive conversation going?

_____

_____

_____

You could state:

- 'Women aren't too emotional to be leaders!'

How can you make this a non-leading and open-ended
question to get a constructive conversation going?

_____

_____

_____

Skill Seven

Persuading with Facts, Stories, and Case Studies

I'd say that among the fundamental purposes of conversations are exchanging information and understanding each other. Communicating to influence decisions and persuade action are examples of taking a conversation to the next level. There are many different techniques to persuade and several factors influence our level of persuasion.

As in sales, the pushy approach is usually not sustainably effective. More successful persuasive approaches include building trust through empathy, signalling our credibility, offering win-win solutions, and clarifying a clear next step. Author Daniel Pink on Masterclass said, 'To be a good persuader, be a decent human being.' He stressed the importance of making the discussion personal and purposeful.

Robert Cialdini's book, *Influence*,[176] is one of my favourite works on the topic. It describes the six principles of influence that help us persuade others: reciprocity, consistency, social proof, liking, authority, and scarcity.

Isn't it interesting how neither Pink nor Cialdini stress that providing the right facts and arguments is key to persuasion. Instead, they focus on the importance of connecting more than anything else.

Connecting starts with uncovering different perspectives and even biases, which may inadvertently be the reason why others object to our arguments. When we're skilled in the art of persuasive communication, we're able to get the other person to listen to us, understand us, and then, convince them to act the way we suggest.

Take the advertisement campaign across the UK around International Women's Day 2022 dubbed 'Imagine'. The posters simply had the short sentences, 'Imagine a CEO. Is it a man?' and 'Imagine someone leaving early to pick up the kids. Is it a woman?' or 'Imagine a nurse. Is it a woman?' No mention of facts or datapoints, and not even a single argument. Still, it is a highly effective advertising campaign that persuaded many commuters— regardless of gender—that they have gender biases. An effective persuasive campaign that went viral, globally.

Let's explore providing facts, data, and case studies versus storytelling.

Research has clearly established that while the human mind struggles to absorb and process data, we respond powerfully to storytelling. Some of the greatest revolutions have been brought about with the aid of skilful storytelling. This is why the story of a baby polar bear cub stranded on a melting glacier with its starving mamma bear is far more effective in raising funds for environmental preservation efforts than loads of scientific data about melting polar caps and rising sea levels.[177] The more the pictures and the story appeal to our emotions, the better they sell our argument. And if it is related to someone like us, and closer to home, as mentioned in the introduction, we relate a little more. Take for instance the flooding in Central Europe in July 2021, which caused 243 deaths. Deadly floods are a yearly returning event in South Asia, but it needed floods in Germany for politicians to get a wake-up call that global warming is real.

We're emotional creatures, and stories engage a different and larger part of our brain. When we're skilled at sharing stories about unfairness, for example, we activate the emotional part of the listener's brain. We paint a picture that appeals to the human senses of seeing, smelling, tasting, hearing, and feeling, activating the sensory areas of the brain as well. As a result, what we say becomes more memorable.[178] Stories are twenty-two times more memorable than facts. And that is a fact.[179]

Nevertheless, research, data, and facts are still important when making the arguments presented in this book. Plus, as in any communication, a lot depends on our audience. As I experience every time I work with consultants, engineers, and financial executives, my stories aren't enough. Some even claim they find storytelling to be a waste of time. They say they want the facts, and they let the facts tell the story. Although people remain social beings and in general are still be affected by stories, the conclusion remains: To be persuasive with a broader group of people, we need both facts and stories.

When it comes to using stories, however, beware: If we're attempting to convince people that women want careers, for example, my story about the woman who got creative about her career goals when imagining she was a man may not be convincing enough. The person we're talking to may know three women who didn't want a career, possibly even within their own family. It's important to think about the possibility that our story may be up against other stories, potentially ones that the other person knows from their own lives. In that case, our story will be reduced to an irrelevant anecdote or even the exception to the rule.

To strengthen our arguments and shatter the myths, adding facts to your stories is important. Especially when we're in a professional setting, providing a business case with positive financial returns will convince many leaders more than the moral case that it's the 'right' thing to do or a stand-alone story.

I had the experience of discussing inclusion with the top leadership of a science-based company. Several of them said they didn't need the business case for inclusion. Instead, they wanted inclusion anchored as a value in their company. Still, this has been the exception. Most leaders are convinced to change their ways when it also makes business sense. If morality would be enough to change the business world, we would not have seen an opioid crisis in the US and nowhere in the world would children be exposed to junk food ads. And as I shared with the group of leaders in the aforementioned science-based company: 'I'd still like you to be clear about your business case for inclusion. I've seen moral shortcuts being made out of convenience when costs and time press us for quick decisions.'

If we realize that we're compromising business results, we're more likely to invest that little extra effort, time, or money in expectation of a positive ROI, compared to when we have morality as the focus. For instance, will we press a third time to see more non-typical candidates for a leadership role when we already have a CV of a suitable, elite-educated man in front of us? We would, if we realized that looking at a broader pool of candidates would result in a 9 percentage points additional EBIT.

Storytelling to persuade

Dr Martin Luther King Jr's 'I have a dream' speech is a wonderful example of using storytelling, with the first paragraphs painting a picture of a crippled 'life of the Negro' and appealing to emotions when he describes that 'the Negro lives on a lonely island of poverty'. The legendary speech, which was a rallying cry for equality and freedom, resulted in the passage of the US Civil Rights Act of 1964, prohibiting discrimination on the basis of race, colour, religion, gender, or national origin. Dr King talked about his dream that one day his children would be judged 'not by the colour of their skin but by the content of their character'.[180]

He personalized the deeply entrenched systemic racism in America and asked the audience to envision what the future could hold for American children.

Storytelling is a psychological tool that's often used in social change movements. Conversations on gender wage gap and the urgent need for pay parity gained momentum when more celebrities and VIPs shared real-life examples of when they were short-changed professionally and economically for being women.

In a 2019 press release, BBC journalist Samira Ahmed stated: 'On the back of my BBC ID card are written the BBC values which include 'we respect each other and celebrate our diversity' and 'we take pride in delivering quality and value for money.' I just ask why the BBC thinks I am worth only a sixth of the value of the work of a man for doing a very similar job.'

Malala Yousafzai's Malala Fund website features her story of how she was shot and miraculously survived to become an education activist in Pakistan and the youngest Nobel Peace Prize laureate. She wrote: 'I spoke out publicly on behalf of girls and our right to learn. And this made me a target. In October 2012, on my way home from school, a masked gunman boarded my school bus and asked, "Who is Malala?" He shot me on the left side of my head. I woke up ten days later in a hospital in Birmingham, England. The doctors and nurses told me about the attack and that people around the world were praying for my recovery.'

The authenticity of these stories adds to the persuasion of the arguments. The transparency and vulnerability increase trust. We can only 'sell' our arguments if we have built trust.

Hard facts

As mentioned previously, to persuade others, it works well to make our arguments specific and add research, data, and facts. For example: 'Women want careers,' isn't as persuasive or convincing as 'According to research, female Harvard Business School graduates set out just as ambitious as their male colleagues. They only differ in one aspect. At the time they graduated from Harvard, more than 75 per cent of men expected that their partners would do the lion's share of childcare, while about 50 per cent of women expected that they would take on the majority of this work. In other words, men expect to be the main breadwinner while women expect to be in a relationship where both are treated as equals. This naturally causes conflict when children arrive. There's more unpaid work to be done, and it's probably the reason why women end up carrying the burden of the unpaid care work, which leaves them with less space and energy to pursue their careers. It isn't that they don't want careers; it's because the system isn't supportive of both parents pursuing demanding careers.'[181]

Case studies of leading companies that have had success with some of the measures suggested in this book also work well. Companies such as Citibank, Microsoft, and Unilever have achieved important milestones in gender equity and inclusion in general. Unilever reached their 50:50 target of gender balance in management in 2019;[182] as mentioned in the introduction, Citibank provided Wallstreet's first female CEO banker in 2020; and Microsoft, a company in a traditionally male-dominated industry, employs 30.7 per cent women in 2022, up from 26.6 per cent in 2018.[183, 184]

Such data and case studies provide what Cialdini called 'social proof'. Leading companies have shown they can do it, providing aspirational but realistic goals for others and good material for persuasion.

Facts tell, stories sell

Brian Tracy, one of my mentors for public speaking, insists on the windshield-wiper method. He says it's effective to deliver facts backed up by stories. For every single fact or argument he delivers, he tells a story. He lives by this in his daily speech too.

When we share facts, we inform. When we tell stories, we move our listeners to action. And when the situation allows us to use both facts and stories, we appeal to almost everyone in the audience regardless of their preferences.

Persuasive strategies in speech

In my 2016 book, *How to Make Yourself Promotable*,[7] I outline four steps to persuasive communication:

- Issue
- Solution
- Benefit
- Next steps.

When we first explain the issue—describing a pain point, a problem, or painting a picture of a better world—we get the attention of those who find it relevant. Next, we move on to our proposed solution and outline the benefits that the solution will bring. If we truly want change, it's helpful to have a clear agreement on the action points that the involved parties will take.

In my first career, which was in corporate communication and advertising, I learned that focussing on benefits is core to advertisement. Professional communicators know that we can only persuade if the audience perceives a benefit. In sales, it's no different, nor is it different in any conversation where we want to 'sell' our idea i.e., persuade.

This is where a lot of people go wrong. They focus too much on their own benefits or don't mention any benefits at all.

---

[7] Available here: https://www.amazon.com/How-Make-Yourself-Promotable-skills-ebook/dp/B01IGYTBKQ

We might mistakenly assume that a solution oozes benefits or that everyone can make their own rational conclusion about benefits. But after two decades in communication, as well as being an entrepreneur, it has become part of my reflex to focus on what's in it for the other person.

Still, I often go wrong by making assumptions about the perspectives of others. For instance, I catch myself in assuming that everyone loves to learn because that's true for me. Or worse, I may think that 'training' is a benefit. This is far from the truth. My clients don't necessarily want training. They want their employees and companies to be successful—usually because they want to be seen as successful themselves—and will only be persuaded to take my services if I'm very specific about how they'll be better off if we close a certain skills gap or change mindsets, leadership styles, and cultures.

Training isn't the answer to 'what's in it for them'. 'Becoming better leaders' is still not seen as the real benefit by all my clients. At least, there are still many bosses and HR departments who are primarily focussed on the business case and receiving a bonus by meeting KPIs (key performance indicators) (although I must admit, more and more companies are also providing training because they want to do good and create good leaders. There is a shift in business from focussing on creating shareholder value to stakeholder value.)

Be clear and concise

Sometimes, less is more. The late US Supreme Court judge Ruth Bader Ginsburg was fantastically short and clear in her messages. When asked by a BBC reporter to explain her reading of then-president Donald Trump's tweet that the Supreme Court could step in to interfere with his impeachment, she could have offered plenty of arguments. Instead, she put it simply: 'Well, the President [Mr Trump] is not a lawyer. He's not law trained.'

She made this highly diplomatic statement while still being clear and concise, what in my words would have been: 'Trump is wrong. He has no clue what he's talking about.'

The power of three

In general, our brain is persuaded when we get three proof points. Let's say we want to convince someone with an open mind that quotas for women should be supported. If we tell a story of one country where it has worked, our listener may dismiss it as a one-off case that's irrelevant to their country. By adding a second country's success story, ideally with different circumstances, our listener may start paying attention. If we add a third slightly different success story, they're much more likely to be convinced.

The reason is that our brain sees a pattern when we've reached three in a row. Just look at the number sequence 2, 4, __? We don't know what comes next. Is it 6? Is it 8? If we see three numbers in sequence—2, 4, 8—we're convinced about the pattern.

Whatever we say after our third 'proof point', however, may weaken our argument. Your listeners got the pattern, and we miss out by compromising brevity.

Exercise

- Think of a recent experience you've had. You can tell the story chronologically: 'I was in a meeting with men only. Rob asked me to fetch coffee, Eugene interrupted me, and Michael presented my idea as his own at the end of the meeting. Luckily, Simon stood up for me.'

  Or you can change it into storytelling: 'When I walked into the meeting room, I realized I was the only woman there. Rob asked me, "Hey, Jane, why don't you get us coffee on your way in?" I coolly ignored the comment. Then, when Eugene interrupted me no less than five times during my presentation, my frustration started to build. What almost made me lose it was when Michael picked up on my idea and made it sound like he'd just thought of it himself! Luckily, Simon chimed in and said, "I'm happy you support Jane's idea, Michael.'"

Try turning your recent experience into a story by describing it as a scene, almost like an act in theatre or a movie, adding some dialogue and evoking some of the senses and describing your feelings.

- When I worked in communications, we constantly focussed on, 'What's in it for the audience.' Every press release, brochure, or advertisement had to stand the test of defining the audience benefit. We loved to use the example of a cold beer. The statement has no benefits. 'Cold' is a feature. The benefit is to relax on a Friday evening after work and bond with friends. In other words, 'providing me the opportunity to relax and bond or socialize' is the benefit.

Of course, in this example, the benefits of a cold beer may be glaringly obvious to beer lovers, but often, this is less obvious and to better persuade, you may want to explicitly state the benefits.

Benefits are best defined when you put yourself in the shoes of the listener. Be relentless in asking yourself the question, 'What's in it for them?' For some, the simple reward of 'doing the right thing' may be enough. Others will need a personal benefit, company benefit, and/or societal benefit.

Choose one of the arguments from the book. How can you add benefits for the listener?

- To practice clarity and brevity, write down what you want to say. Edit it by cutting out every single word that doesn't add value. This helps you sharpen your skills in both writing and spoken language. Emails are a great way of practising this skill because you can delete every word that doesn't add any value before hitting 'send'.
- Watch a video on MetaMind Training's YouTube channel to understand the power of using three proof points.[185]

Skill Eight

Managing Confrontations

There's no question that women's opinions are often dismissed, and women are interrupted more frequently than men. Yet, we have the same right to be heard. Indra Nooyi, the former CEO of PepsiCo and current board member of Amazon, has been quoted to have said, 'Don't say "I'll talk to him outside the meeting." Right there, stop the meeting.'[186] She's referring to speaking up immediately when we're dismissed as women. I agree with this in many situations, especially if you have a certain amount of power or if you work in a company that's open.

However, speaking up about a misogynist comment is risky depending on where we work and our position in the company. A friend of mine recently shared that she was seen as 'too sensitive' about 'innocent locker-room talk'. She's an emancipated woman who expects to be treated fairly, and she regularly calls out misogynistic comments. Yet, she works in a conservative country, in a conservative industry, and for a conservative company. She says she's sometimes seen as an extreme feminist for calling out behaviours that are so outdated, I haven't seen them in my environment for the better part of a decade. The sad truth is that she isn't in the same position as Indra Nooyi and can only push the boundaries so far if she still wants to be taken seriously . . . and keep her job.

There are many different imaginable situations where 'stopping the meeting' won't help us advance fairness. How we manage confrontations needs to be adjusted to the circumstances.

I was once told a story about a woman who was on the receiving end of sarcastic, misogynistic remarks in a meeting. Afterwards, one of the men said he was a bit surprised she hadn't stood up for herself because, as he said, 'your values were violated.' She replied, 'I'm a bit surprised that you didn't stand up for me because I thought your values were also violated.'

Groups at a disadvantage need all the support they can get. It's easier to stand up for the 'weak', or let's just say less privileged, when we're part the demographic group that holds the most power, for instance, a man in a male-dominated organization. When we observe others being interrupted, especially when they have less privilege than us, or when others are the brunt of inappropriate jokes, or any number of other 'microaggressions', we must gather courage to call out the behaviour. It's easier and is much more powerful when others are standing up for us.

Towards that end, if we seek allies who are in the powerful group and educate them on how they can support us, someone else can handle some of the confrontations on our behalf. This isn't to say that it's our responsibility to seek allies or that women should look to men to 'come to our rescue'. Rather, it's at least as much the responsibility of in-power groups to stop violations of fairness. When we are in a position of less power, we can help raise awareness about the effectiveness of allyship by raising the unfairness in a separate conversation.

Handling confrontations in practice

When you've been labelled the 'irrational' or 'unreasonable' feminist, or even the 'feminazi', you can, of course, opt to be sterner or raise your voice louder. You can also choose your battles wisely. People have been passed over for promotions because they were considered too 'difficult', so your best option is to use your judgement in your specific situation. Sometimes, there's a good argument for working with the system and changing it from within. Weigh this against doing 'the right thing'.

Remember Huffington from the section we discussed myth about women speaking too much? She was able to call out Bonderman because she had power. Bonderman first apologized and later resigned.

If you're in a position to speak up, please do so. I'm by no means advocating the suppression of voices that speak up for fairness. Huffington shows that we can make a difference, in this case, create awareness, by speaking up. And I want to embolden you by stressing that sometimes, you have more power than you realize.

Momoko Nojo, a then twenty-two-year-old student in Japan,[187] discovered this when she launched an online petition against the Tokyo Olympics chief Yoshiro Mori for misogynist remarks similar to those made at Uber. He said, 'If we increase the number of female board members, we have to make sure their speaking time is restricted somewhat; they have difficulty finishing, which is annoying.'[188] He implied that women as a whole are unfocussed, unprofessional, and waste other executives' time. Nojo's campaign helped force Mori, a former prime minister, to resign.

In another eloquent confrontation, Julia Gillard, then prime minister of Australia, called out Tony Abbott, the opposition leader, for being sexist.[189] She talked resolutely about Abbott's comments for several minutes, and the message landed. An Australian scholar called Gillard's short speech a 'watershed moment' and said they were 'relieved that she had actually named what was happening'.[190]

I sincerely hope everyone has the standing to call out such offences and stop the sexist narratives. In Gillard's case, there were a number of issues, including calling her 'a man's b****'. But I'm also well aware that doing what Nooyi, Huffington, and Gillard did could, in the worst case, cost you your job. That's why I've provided various strategies for shattering these narratives— some more confrontational than others.

'A lot of people will be wondering, are you two meeting just because you're similar in age and, you know, got a lot of common stuff there,' a reporter from New Zealand asked his Prime Minsiter Jacinda Ardern at a joint press conference with Finnish Prime Minister Sanna Marin.

'My first question is I wonder whether or not anyone ever asked [former US President] Barack Obama and [former New Zealand Prime Minister] John Key if they met because they were of similar age"' Ardern interjected quickly. 'We of course have a high proportion of men in politics. It's reality. Because two women meet, it is not just simply because of their gender.' She went on to quote export statistics, technology, and the huge potential in collaboration. 'Yes, we are meeting because we are prime ministers,' Marin added.

Quickly rejecting the sexist or ignorant comment, and moving on to what's important, is the strategy that the two prime ministers pursued, which was more subtle than Gillard's confrontation.

I can't stress enough: If you happen to be a man reading this, or you're in the dominant in-group, the most powerful thing you can do is be an ally or advocate on behalf of those who suffer unfair treatment and speak up. Point out the unfairness. Have the conversation. Make clear that the behaviour is unacceptable and model the right behaviour.

If your combat gloves are on and you're ready for the confrontations, however, the next chapter is for you.

Exercise

Write down three situations that you find unjust and would like to see improved.

1.
2.
3.

Which of these, if any, do you believe you have the power to influence, while also keeping your job and/or reputation? How can you gather support from others in the in-power group? What can you do now or next time to make a bigger difference? Make notes on each.

1.
2.
3.

Skill Nine

Healthy Debates

Whether to debate and challenge another's opinion depends on many factors, including your own appetite for it and your comfort with conflict, the environment, the mindset of the other person participating in the debate, the communication skills of all parties involved, and the potential for compromise in the situation.

Some companies have focussed strongly on building 'psychological safety'—i.e., the absence of interpersonal fear, which ensures that everybody feels safe to speak up about workplace-relevant content. If you're in a psychologically safe environment, you have the best preconditions to immerse yourself in debates.

A McKinsey report states: 'To boost psychological safety at work, leaders must first turn inward to understand and integrate their own emotions and fears, and then turn outward to support others.'[191] Engaging in a healthy debate is much the same. Self-awareness as well as turning outward with empathy and compassion are key.

Debating can be a healthy way to advance a discussion. When challenging viewpoints, we can explore further and broaden our minds. When presented with different opinions, we apply critical thinking and are invited to see the world in a different light. If we take away the egos and the emotions as well as the miscommunication from challenging conversations, all that's left are different opinions and stances. We can explore the optimal solution and be inspired by each other. Wouldn't that result in a wonderful, enlightening discussion and accelerated progress?

Of course, the difference in people's appetite for challenging conversations, uncovering opposing opinions, and even the need for harmony can be a big obstacle. Some people may have a low appetite and may withdraw. Others may not want to argue against those in power. Some may find it difficult to separate the issue from the person and personally offend or become personally offended during a debate. Others may not feel they can find the right arguments as fast as their counterparts, constantly feeling vulnerable and in a weak position, and consequently dislike debate entirely.

I-statements to ease tensions

You may have heard how 'I-statements' avoid escalation of emotions. It's a basic principle of a healthy debate—to make sure it's about the issue and potentially about how we feel, not attacking our counterpart.

For example, 'You offend me,' is a 'you-statement' that accuses someone else of wrongdoing. I-statements, on the other hand, add our perspective or feelings. In this case, we would say, 'I feel offended when interrupted,' not 'I feel you have offended me,' which is still accusatory. Note, however, that some people struggle to accept either way of speaking. On various occasions, I've heard participants in our Women in Leadership programmes say, 'My boss said "I don't care about your feelings," and "Leave your feelings at home with your family."' Not all leaders have EQ and human decency.

Communication advice, again, is never fool proof. We all have our subjective communication preferences.

The bottom-line of the learning doesn't change. We're more likely to be successful if we approach debates with a constructive attitude, focus on the issue, look for a win-win solution, and share our perspective, as well as stay open to the other person's perspective. When we focus on finding areas of agreement and validate each other's positive contributions, other topics can be discussed with a greater likelihood of positive results.

Boxing versus dancing

Recall our previous discussion about 'boxing' versus 'dancing'. When you choose to debate, you can listen to the other person's cues and build on them (dancing) or knock the other party out (boxing). You may argue that sometimes, people need a knockout to wake them up. But let's focus on how to build trust and engage in constructive communication.

'You always interrupt me,' is a boxing move and not recommended. The other person will probably get defensive and send back a retaliatory blow that takes the conversation nowhere.

Instead, we can say, 'I felt frustrated because I was interrupted a handful of times during the meeting.' This I-statement with a focus on the issue rather than a personal attack invites the other person to respond in a more constructive way. It encourages them to see and understand us. It's more of a dance.

'This won't work,' or 'You're a misogynist' are additional examples of boxing. A possible reaction from the other person to the latter might be, 'I promoted a woman into leadership last year!'

You've just entered the boxing ring.

How can we change these sentences to dance moves?

How about: 'What's needed in order to make this work?' Or, 'What's needed to promote more women into leadership?' Note, again, my favourite technique of asking questions, which serve as an invitation to dance.

Certain words are an invitation to a boxing match. Anything that accuses, for instance, such as generalizations:

- You always . . .
- You never . . .
- Men don't . . .
- Women won't . . .

Negative words or sentences that imply the other person is wrong are also likely to end up in a boxing match:

- But . . .
- No . . .
- That's impossible . . .

Instead, how about:

- I appreciate it when . . .
- I see the benefits of . . .
- Women have a stronger tendency to . . .
- How about we try to . . .
- Yes, and what's more . . .

Traditional debate usually brings out the logical fallacies of the other side. As we do this, it's good to be aware of the fallacies and weaknesses in our own argument and prepare ourselves to address them. If we think of a healthy debate as an exercise in critical thinking, we'll be able to distinguish between the issue and the other person. We'll moderate our emotions so that we can respond rather than react.

Exercise

Think about a debate from your past during which you became upset.

- Did you become upset about the issue, the difference in opinion, or something personal, such as how you were treated? Did you feel upset because you didn't get to 'win' the discussion?
- What was the issue? Separating the issue from the people involved is essential to successful debating.

Write down the issue:

_____

_____

_____

Is there anything that shows that the real issue was interpersonal? For instance: 'He didn't listen,' or 'I'm so upset that he doesn't respect women.' Can you analyse again, and write what the issue was?

_____

_____

_____

In improv theatre, dialogues are not scripted and rather spontaneously build on each other. The actors take turns adding a line or an idea. A great exercise that is taken from improv is to experience what kind of response provides a constructive dialogue, and how to kill a dialogue. In improv, you depend on your co-actors providing constructive dialogue, or you all fail on stage.

Get a buddy for this exercise and pretend to plan activities for your company's ERGs together. Any brainstorming idea can work. Say, you start with the mere suggestion of planning activities for next year. Your buddy answers by saying, 'No, but . . .' You continue relentlessly with the suggestion of planning activities to bring more structure to your grass root activities and start the sentence with 'No, but . . .' Take turns adding to each other, every time starting with 'No, but . . .' Before two minutes have passed, you're likely to be exhausted and done, probably even somewhat frustrated. For instance:

You: 'Let's do some activity planning together for the ERG. I suggest we have monthly lunch-and-learn sessions.'

Buddy: 'No, but lunch-and-learn is too work-intensive. We need to arrange lunch and we don't have a budget.'

You: 'No, but we could do with some inspiration from experts.'

Buddy: 'No, but . . .' etc.

Next, you repeat the exercise, and you start every sentence with 'Yes, and . . .' For instance:

You: 'Let's do some activity planning together for the ERG. I suggest we have monthly lunch-and-learn sessions!'

Buddy: 'Yes, and let's have people bring their own lunches since we don't have a budget.'

You: 'Yes, and . . .' etc.

Which round was more fun and productive?

Even when writing the role plays above, I can immediately feel how I become more creative. Our creative thinking is appealed to because we become solution-oriented.

You can do another round, starting your turn with 'Yes, I love your idea about the party, and we could also . . .' See how it changes when you find something to like in the other person's argument and give them praise before providing your own idea.

Isn't 'Yes, and . . .' the ultimate conversation dancing technique, allowing us to let go of the need to be right or making the other person wrong?

Skill Ten

Understanding the Cultural Dimension

In Asia, which I currently call home, people tend to be more reluctant to speak their minds than in Denmark, where I was born, and especially the Netherlands, where I grew up. As most Asians will have heard from a grandparent: 'You have two ears, two eyes, and one mouth. Use them proportionally.'

Western education systems are, to varying degrees, focussed on debating, sharing, and presenting in front of the class.

In France, an intensive debate is seen as advancing the cause, and the topic is clearly separated from the person making the argument. In essays, children are taught to produce a thesis, antithesis, and synthesis. They make a point, make a case against, and summarize their conclusions. As a natural consequence of using this approach for every single essay and scientific report throughout their education, it becomes a habit in daily conversation. We can see people discussing politics with passion and remaining friends, which sadly has become a rarity in the US. This is despite their education system training children from kindergarten to speak up in front of the class, for instance with 'show and tell', where four-year-olds may take a toy or pet to school and share about the topic.

The traditional Asian education system is in stark contrast to most western ones and much more based on listening, which has a profound impact on our communication style and appetite for debates.

Hierarchy also plays a role. Asian cultures are in general more hierarchical than most western cultures. As a result, people who consider themselves to be of lower status usually only speak up when asked. Even in psychologically safe environments, many Asians spend less time speaking during meetings than your average Westerners.

Of course, marginalized or under-represented demographic groups may also feel their opinions are less valued and, therefore, become reluctant in sharing their true beliefs.

The hesitancy of lower-power groups to speak up in meetings is a challenge for both multinational companies and their employees.

In a recent meeting with very senior Asian executives, logo design was the first point on the agenda. As I've mentioned, in my first career, I worked in advertising and corporate communication, so I had much more experience and expertise in this area than the rest of the group. Since it was my first meeting with this team, I had no idea who was responsible for creating the logo, and I certainly didn't want to risk criticizing and distancing a group far more senior than myself within the first five minutes of acquaintance.

Instead of sharing what I thought was wrong with the logo, I asked, 'What would you like to achieve and communicate with this logo?' The open-ended question steered the discussion in the right direction. Often, we can make a statement that's much more welcome than 'I'm an expert in this field, and I will tell you . . .' The team reflected on my question and turned to me, after which we had a discussion that was more fruitful than one that would have focussed on 'this works' and 'that doesn't'. I managed to avoid distancing myself from a group from a different culture and gained their ears simply by listening, assessing the situation, stepping back, and asking an open-ended question. And let me tell you, I was very relieved by how well it went!

Another difference in communication is how directly we express ourselves—in other words, how quickly and frankly we get to our point. An Indian friend shared how she caught herself telling a taxi driver that 'most drivers take a U-turn here', rather than directly instructing him to take a U-turn. Her cultural upbringing had taught her to phrase her opinions indirectly in order to avoid offending anyone, even in situations where she was clearly the expert, such as finding her way home. This is so deeply rooted that even in casual conversations and after having established herself as a highly educated expert, she says that she still catches herself not stating facts or opinion in a clear manner.

Cultural intelligence—how to skilfully navigate cultures—would require an entire book in its own right. Simply observing, understanding, and modifying our approach to take cultural nuances into account can help immensely in navigating challenging conversations.

Ways to keep cultural differences in mind

For those who want to gather the courage to speak up more, I suggest starting with open-ended questions like the ones above. Questions seem less imposing, especially in Asian culture, when the natural tendency is to ask rather than tell. When you begin to feel more at ease about sharing your opinions directly, you can go on to the next stage and prepare statements before their meetings.

The technique of asking questions works equally well when we're hesitant to speak up for other reasons, such as, our perception of being less important than others in the room. That was my situation in the meeting about the logo.

Nevertheless, I can't stress enough that I'm not trying to discourage you from voicing your opinion. I wish for every organization to have an abundance of psychological safety and for every employee to have the courage and skills to speak up regardless of their demographic group.

However, I see a different reality in almost every company I work with, especially in Asia. That's one important reason why I'm a big fan of asking questions.

It's also helpful to keep in mind different communication styles that are based on culture. In meetings in some countries and cultures in Asia, an efficient manager may not correct the top leader even if the leader is wrong. This is because honour or saving face is important, so it would be considered disrespectful to contradict a boss in public. Knowing this context helps because then we can do any fact-checking discreetly.

Recently, someone on my team asked me, 'Have you paid Adele?'

My first thought was, 'Why on earth are you asking me? I'm a few levels more senior than you, and you have access to the bank statements. Are you expecting me to remember the hundreds of payments I've made since Adele's invoice came in six months ago? It's your job. Please take responsibility for your own area of work and let me focus on more higher value work.'

Now, of course, knowing the Southeast Asian indirect communication style, I quickly realized that what she actually meant was, 'Mette, you forgot to pay Adele. Please pay her.' A lot can be lost in translation, causing unnecessary misunderstandings and conflicts, and dismissing talent. Taking cultural differences into account can keep those to a minimum.

Exercise

Think of a discussion you had or have heard about gender equality with someone from a different culture.

- How could culture have affected the discussion?
- Keeping in mind the preference for confrontation/ directness or vice versa, is there anything you can do to contribute or do better next time?

Postscript

There were many instances in corporate life where I felt that I didn't 'fit in'. Like many other women, I was dismissed. I was simply not considered for a career promotion by those who would take the decisions. Of course, I have been supported and liked by individual bosses—but what do great performance ratings and appreciation matter if they do not change the mindset of key stakeholders that the husband is the primary career person? I would be given jobs to keep me busy, rather than fulfilled by growing into the best person I could be and doing meaningful work. From starting with a strong self-belief that I could have a career, my confidence was diminished every time I was not taken seriously, every time the men around me had an easier time getting promoted or salary increases, and every time I was told I had to start over again and prove what I could do rather than giving me opportunities based on my potential. In other words, the typical ways that women have obstacles put in their path in addition to obstacles that any straight, able-bodied, men of mainstream ethnicity would be confronted with.

After years of facing the obstacles, I did start to have unhealthy self-doubts. I probably needed the identity shift that I could be a leader. I had it during university and while doing my MBA, even when I started out in the high potential management development programme—but I lost confidence every single time I was dismissed. Some people are born rebels and get more stubborn for every 'no' they get. I'm like most women. I started telling myself stories that I probably didn't have what it takes to make it to the executive leadership team.

I've been on the receiving end of several of the stories in this book, and I have heard many of them in professional environments. One of the more nonsensical things that I heard in my corporate career that hasn't been covered in this book is, 'If we promote her and she fails, we will set a bad precedent and make it very difficult for all other women.' I thought it was just the company I worked for, when I heard it repeated in a completely different time and place. Yes, if a woman fails, it is because she is a woman. If a man fails, it is because an individual was not up to it.

I just can't leave the topic alone. I want to give women who are still subject to such unfairness the confidence that they are okay. It's the stories that we keep on telling and the culture that is created, in addition to the systems, processes, and mindsets—including our own—that are unhelpful.

I sometimes say, 'I don't care about women,' which of course needs to be in the context that I wish that gender—whatever gender—wouldn't matter. Just like I wish that it wouldn't matter what ability, nationality, ethnicity, sexual orientation, identity, and much else you are labelled with or identify as. I care about people (and women happen to be people). I care about fairness. And I do hope that my experience and perspectives can make the world a little bit more equal for all. I wish it didn't have to be about women, but unfortunately, it still is.

The idea of the book came up in a workshop with a client where we discussed some of the strange stories that get a life of their own. And in my work, I discovered that every organization has these stories. That's when I decided I needed to collect them and write a book about these. We must dispel these narratives, these stories, these myths that undermine women and are holding them back from flourishing at work.

It's my sincere hope that creating both awareness about the narratives and sharing research-based true stories as well as arguments and tools to shatter them will help move the needle just a little on gender balance.

Acknowledgements

Writing a book is team effort. I couldn't have done it without the help of my entire team, both at MetaMind and at KeyNote Women Speakers. I get loads of inspiration from all of you on a daily basis!

My clients also play a big role—the idea of this book came during an Inclusive Leadership intervention with the AAA leadership team at Barilla—a company which is highly dedicated to diversity and inclusion. Many other clients have contributed to this—knowingly and unknowingly.

The interviews in this book are core to making this book readable—thank you to all of you who have shared openly with me, whether under your own name or anonymously. There were many other people whose stories and viewpoints were central to the conceptual development of this book, but whose stories only made it indirectly. I'm still very grateful to the time you have spent with me sharing your views and your experiences.

A previous business partner, Kaumudi Goda, provided excellent support and great insights into the early phases of this book. Anna Alberti provided great inspiration for a lot of the content, as did Shehara Viswanathan. My previous editor, Tanja Gardner, helped structure the book concept, and Melanie Votaw ironed out some language along the way.

My faithful content researcher for almost a decade, Vita Dizon is responsible together with Flavia Vicari for ensuring the book is based on sound research.

And, of course, my core family, Axel, Louca, and Leon, for proofreading, providing commentary, and supporting me throughout this project.

And, finally, the team at Penguin Random House: the publisher, Nora Nazerene Abu Bakar, the editor, Surina Jain, the proofreader, Sneha Bhagwat, and Divya Gaur, who did the cover design, as well as Amberdawn Manaois and Rupal Vyas. Thank you, couldn't have done it without you!

Endnotes

Some interlocutors requested for their identities to be withheld. Names marked with a * have therefore been changed to protect their privacy.

1. Mehrabian, Albert, and Susan V. Ferris. 1967. 'Inference of Attitudes From Nonverbal Communication in Two Channels.' *Journal of Consulting Psychology*, vol. 31, no. 3, pp. 248–52. https://doi.org/10.1037/h0024648. (Accessed July 6, 2023)

2. 'Common Sense Is Nothing More Than a Deposit of Prejudices Laid Down in the Mind Before Age Eighteen.' *Quote Investigator.* https://quoteinvestigator.com/2014/04/29/common-sense. (Accessed July 6, 2023)

3. Kahneman, Daniel. 2011. *Thinking, Fast and Slow.* Farrar, Straus and Giroux

4. Hinchliffe, Emma. 2022 'Women CEOs run 10.4% of Fortune 500 companies. A quarter of the 52 leaders became CEO in the last year.' *Fortune.* https://fortune.com/2023/06/05/fortune-500-companies-2023-women-10-percent. (Accessed July 6, 2023)

5. 'Women in the Changing World of Work - Facts You Should Know.' *UN Women.* https://interactive.unwomen.org/multimedia/infographic/changingworldofwork/en/index.html. (Accessed December 25, 2020)

6.   'Women at Work – Trends 2016.' *International Labour Organization*. https://www.ilo.org/wcmsp5/groups/public/---dgreports/---dcomm/---publ/documents/publication/wcms_457317.pdf. (Accessed December 25, 2020)

7.   'Women in the Changing World of Work - Facts You Should Know.' *UN Women*. https://interactive.unwomen.org/multimedia/infographic/changingworldofwork/en/index.html. (Accessed December 25, 2020)

8.   Antilla, Susan. 2022. 'Stark Lessons From Wall Street's #MeToo Moment.' *The Intercept*. https://theintercept.com/2019/10/07/metoo-wall-street-sexual-harassment-arbitration. (Accessed July 7, 2023)

9.   Stop Street Harassment. '2018 Study on Sexual Harassment and Assault.' https://stopstreetharassment.org/our-work/nationalstudy/2018-national-sexual-abuse-report. (Accessed July 6, 2023)

10.   Oppenheim, Maya. 2020. 'Employers urging women to dress 'sexier' in video meetings, study finds.' *The Independent*. https://www.independent.co.uk/news/uk/home-news/video-calls-women-sexier-dress-employers-a9633056.html. (Accessed July 6, 2023)

11.   Refer to endnote 8.

12.   'Citi CEO Michael Corbat Announces Plans to Retire in February 2021, Board of Directors Selects Jane Fraser to Succeed Corbat as CEO.' *Citi Group*. www.citigroup.com/global/news/press-release/2020/citi-ceo-michael-corbat-announces-plans-to-retire-in-february-2021-board-of-directors-selects-jane-fraser-to-succeed-corbat-as-ceo. (Accessed July 6, 2023)

13.   'She's Asking for It [Video].' *British Comedy Guide*. https://comedy.co.uk/online/videos/20872/shes-asking-for-it. (Accessed July 6, 2023)

14. Pradhan, Rabindra Kumar, et al. 2017. 'Purpose, Passion, and Performance at the Workplace: Exploring the Nature, Structure, and Relationship.' *The Psychologist-Manager Journal*, vol. 20, no. 4. https://doi.org/10.1037/mgr0000059. (Accessed July 6, 2023)

15. 'Case study: Always #LikeAGirl.' 2015. *Campaign*. https://www.campaignlive.co.uk/article/case-study-always-likeagirl/1366870. (Accessed Aug 7, 2023)

16. TEDx Talks. 'Dare to Lead Like a Girl | Dalia Feldheim | TEDxJaffaWomen [Video].' YouTube. https://youtube.com/watch?v=nAUIJlAhW5c. (Accessed July 6, 2023)

17. Frasca, Teresa, et al. 2022. 'Words Like Weapons: Labeling Women as Emotional During a Disagreement Negatively Affects the Perceived Legitimacy of Their Arguments.' *Psychology of Women Quarterly*, vol. 46, no. 4. https://doi.org/10.1177/03616843221123745. (Accessed July 6, 2023)

18. 'The Double-Bind Dilemma for Women in Leadership.' *Catalyst*. https://catalyst.org/research/infographic-the-double-bind-dilemma-for-women-in-leadership. (Accessed July 6, 2023)

19. Marshburn, Christopher K., et al. 2020. 'Workplace Anger Costs Women Irrespective of Race.' *Frontiers in Psychology*, vol. 11. https://doi.org/10.3389/fpsyg.2020.579884. (Accessed July 6, 2023)

20. 'Professionalism.' *Oxford Advanced Learner's Dictionary*. https://oxford learnersdictionaries.com/definition/english/professionalism?q=professionalism. (Accessed July 6, 2023)

21. Collier, Lorna. 2014. 'Why We Cry.' *American Psychological Association*. https://apa.org/monitor/2014/02/cry. (Accessed July 6, 2023)

22. 'All Emotions Are Information.' *WISE*. https://wise-qatar.org/brackett-emotional-intelligence-yale. (Accessed July 6, 2023)

23. The Atlantic. 'Is It Okay to Cry at Work? [Video].' YouTube. https://youtube.com/watch?v=1LHxi7oFnyw. (Accessed July 6, 2023)

24. Refer to endnote 21.

25. Carnevale, Anthony P., et al. 2019. 'May the Best Woman Win? Education and Bias against Women in American Politics.' *Georgetown University Center for Education and the Workforce.* https://cew.georgetown.edu/wp-content/uploads/ Women_in_Politics.pdf. (Accessed July 6, 2023)

26. Kantar Public. 'The Reykjavik Index for Leadership.' https:// reykjavikforum.global/wp-content/uploads/2019/06/ reykjavik-index-2021-1.pdf. (Accessed July 6, 2023)

27. Ekman, Paul, 'What Is Anger? | Feeling Anger.' https:// paulekman.com/universal-emotions/what-is-anger/. (Accessed July 6, 2023)

28. Mestre, María Vicenta Samper, Paula Frías, María Dolores Tur, Ana María. 2009. 'Are women more empathetic than men? A longitudinal study in adolescence.' *APA PsycNet.* https://psycnet.apa.org/record/2009-07459-008. (Accessed Jul 6, 2023)

29. 'Eight Surprising Reasons Women Are Actually Happier at Work Than Men.' *Ellevate.* https://www.ellevatenetwork. com/articles/9201-eight-surprising-reasons-women-are-actually-happier-at-work-than-men. (Accessed August 7, 2023)

30. Goleman, Daniel. 1995. *Emotional Intelligence.* Bantam Books.

31. NBC News. 'Full Transcript of Zelenskyy's Emotional Appeal to Russians.' https://nbcnews.com/news/world/ full-transcript-zelenskyys-emotional-appeal-russians-rcna17485. (Accessed July 6, 2023)

32. Heath, Kathryn. 2018. 'How Women Can Show Passion at Work Without Seeming "Emotional"'.*Harvard Business Review.* https://hbr.org/2015/09/how-women-can-show-passion-at-work-without-seeming-emotional. (Accessed July 6, 2023)

33. 'The Anglo-Dutch Translation Guide.' *Reddit*. https://reddit.com/r/thenetherlands/comments/2iz0go/the_anglodutch_translation_guide. (Accessed July 6, 2023)

34. Woetzel, Jonathan, Anu Madgavkar, Kweilin Ellingrud, Eric Labaye, Sandrine Devillard, Eric Kutcher, James Manyika, Richard Dobbs, and Mekala Krishnan. 2015. 'The Power of Parity: How Advancing Women's Equality Can Add $12 Trillion to Global Growth.' *McKinsey Global Institute*. https://www.mckinsey.com/featured-insights/employment-and-growth/how-advancing-womens-equality-can-add-12-trillion-to-global-growth. (Accessed July 6, 2023)

35. Gorman, Elizabeth H., and Julie A. Kmec. 2007. 'We (Have to) Try Harder.' *Gender & Society*, vol. 21, no. 6. https://doi.org/10.1177/0891243207309900. (Accessed July 6, 2023)

36. Chamorro-Premuzic, Tomas. 'Why Do so Many Incompetent Men Become Leaders?' *Harvard Business Review*. February 27, 2023. hbr.org/2013/08/why-do-so-many-incompetent-men%E2%80%94. (Accessed August 7, 2023)

37. Chamorro-Premuzic, Tomas. 'Why Do so Many Incompetent Men Become Leaders?' YouTube. March 26, 2019. www.youtube.com/watch?v=zeAEFEXvcBg. (Accessed August 7, 2023)

38. Bowley, Rachel. 2017. 'Women's Equality Day: A Look At Women in The Workplace in 2017.' *LinkedIn Official Blog*. https://blog.linkedin.com/2017/august/28/womens-equality-day-a-look-at-women-in-the-workplace-in-2017. (Accessed July 6, 2023)

39. Jennifer Roche. 2019. 'Women Persistently Sell Themselves Short of Same-Skill Men.' *National Bureau of Economic Research*. https://www.nber.org/digest/dec19/women-persistently-sell-themselves-short-same-skill-men. (Accessed July 6, 2023)

40. Zenger, Jack and Joseph Folkman. 2019. 'Research: Women Score Higher Than Men in Most Leadership Skills.' *Harvard Business Review*. https://hbr.org/2019/06/research-women-

score-higher-than-men-in-most-leadership-skills. (Accessed July 6, 2023)

41. O'Dea, R. E., M. Lagisz, M. D. Jennions, and S. Nakagawa. 2018. 'Gender Differences in Individual Variation in Academic Grades Fail to Fit Expected Patterns for STEM.' *Nature News.* https://www.nature.com/articles/s41467-018-06292-0. (Accessed July 6, 2023)

42. Francesconi, Marco, and Matthias Parey. 2018. 'Early Gender Gaps Among University Graduates.' European Economic Review, vol. 109. pp. 63–82. https://doi.org/10.1016/j.euroecorev.2018.02.004. (Accessed July 6, 2023)

43. Marcus, Jon. 2021. 'In One Country, Women Now Outnumber Men in College by Two to One.' *The Hechinger Report.* https://hechingerreport.org/in-one-country-women-now-outnumber-men-in-college-by-two-to-one. (Accessed July 6, 2023)

44. 'Education at a Glance 2019.' *Organisation for Economic Co-operation and Development.* https://oecd-ilibrary.org/education/education-at-a-glance-2019_f8d7880d-en. (Accessed July 6, 2023)

45. Refer to endnote 40.

46. Niaura, Dominykas. 2019. 'Teacher Uses Band-Aids To Explain Difference Between Equality Vs Equity, 8-Year-Olds Understand It Better Than Adults.' *Bored Panda.* https://boredpanda.com/equality-equity-band-aid-student-lesson (Accessed July 6, 2023)

47. Lorenzo, Rocío, Nicole Voigt, Miki Tsusaka, Matt Krentz, and Katie Abouzahr. 2018. 'How Diverse Leadership Teams Boost Innovation.' *BCG Global.* https://bcg.com/publications/2018/how-diverse-leadership-teams-boost-innovation. (Accessed July 6, 2023)

48. Rock, David. 2019. 'Why Diverse Teams Are Smarter.' *Harvard Business Review*. https://hbr.org/2016/11/why-diverse-teams-are-smarter. (Accessed July 6, 2023)

49. Sandberg, Sheryl, and Adam Grant. 2016. 'Sheryl Sandberg on the Myth of the Catty Woman.' *The New York Times*. https://nytimes.com/2016/06/23/opinion/sunday/sheryl-sandberg-on-the-myth-of-the-catty-woman.html. (Accessed July 6, 2023)

50. 'Myths About Gossip Busted: Study Explores Nuances of Who Gossips, and What They Gossip About.' *ScienceDaily*. https://sciencedaily.com/releases/2019/05/190503100814.htm. (Accessed July 6, 2023)

51. Kramer, Andrea and Harris, Alton. 2019. 'The Persistent Myth of Female Office Rivalries.' *Harvard Business Review*. https://hbr.org/2019/12/the-persistent-myth-of-female-office-rivalries. (Accessed July 6, 2023)

52. Blau, Francine D., and Jed DeVaro. 2007. 'New Evidence on Gender Differences in Promotion Rates: An Empirical Analysis of a Sample of New Hires.' *Industrial Relations*, vol. 46, no. 3. https://doi.org/10.1111/j.1468-232x.2007.00479.x. (Accessed July 6, 2023)

53. Zhao, Sophia and Maw-Der Foo. 2020. 'Queen Bee Syndrome The Real Reason Women Do Not Promote Women.' *Center for Creative Leadership*. http://cclinnovation.org/wp-content/uploads/2020/03/queen-bee-syndrome.pdf. (Accessed July 6, 2023)

54. Stranden, Anne Lise. 2022. 'Does Imposing Women's Quotas for Corporate Boards Pay Off?' *ScienceNorway*. https://sciencenorway.no/economy-gender-gender-and-society/does-imposing-womens-quotas-for-corporate-boards-pay-off/. (Accessed July 6, 2023)

55. 'Diversity Wins: How Inclusion Matters.' *McKinsey & Company.* https://www.mckinsey.com/featured-insights/diversity-and-inclusion/diversity-wins-how-inclusion-matters. (Accessed July 7, 2023)

56. 'Diverse Boards Haven't Led to Diverse Leadership Teams (Yet).' *The Boston Consulting Group.* https://www.bcg.com/publications/2020/diverse-leadership-teams. (Accessed July 6, 2023)

57. 'The Mix That Matters Innovation Through Diversity.' *The Boston Consulting Group.* https://media-publications.bcg.com/22feb2017-mix-that-matters.pdf. (Accessed July 7, 2023)

58. Refer to endnote 55

59. Credit Suisse Research Institute. 'The CS Gender 3000: The Reward for Change.' https://evolveetfs.com/wp-content/uploads/2017/08/Credit-Suisse-Reward-for-Change_1495660293279_2.pdf. (Accessed July 7, 2023)

60. 'Global Gender Gap Report 2022.' *World Economic Forum.* https://www.weforum.org/reports/global-gender-gap-report-2022. (Accessed July 7, 2023)

61. Wagner, Ines. 'How Iceland Is Closing the Gender Wage Gap.' *Harvard Business Review,* January 8, 2021, www.hbr.org/2021/01/how-iceland-is-closing-the-gender-wage-gap. (Accessed July 7, 2023)

62. John, Tara. 2018. 'Iceland Makes Equal Pay the Law.' *Time.* https://time.com/5087354/iceland-makes-equal-pay-the-law/. (Accessed July 7, 2023)

63. 'Gender Pay Gap Data.' *Workplace Gender Equality Agency.* www.wgea.gov.au/publications/australias-gender-pay-gap-statistics. (Accessed July 7, 2023)

64. 'Singapore's Adjusted Gender Pay Gap Narrows to 6%.' *Ministry of Manpower.* www.mom.gov.sg/newsroom/press-releases/2020/0109-singapores-adjusted-gender-pay-gap-narrows-to-6-percent. (Accessed July 7, 2023)

65. 'Global Gender Gap Report 2020.' *World Economic Forum.*
    https://www3.weforum.org/docs/WEF_GGGR_2020.
    pdf. (Accessed July 7, 2023)
66. 'Global Gender Gap Report 2023.' *World Economic Forum.*
    https://www3.weforum.org/docs/WEF_GGGR_2023.
    pdf. (Accessed July 7, 2023)
67. Andersen, Torben. 2020. '50 år gammelt lønsystem fryser
    kvindefag fast på lave lønninger.' *Mandag Morgen.* https://
    www.mm.dk/artikel/50-aar-gammelt-loensystem-fryser-
    kvindefag-fast-paa-lave-loenninger. (Accessed July 6, 2023)
68. Mandell, Andrea. 2018. 'Exclusive: Wahlberg got $1.5M
    for "All the Money" reshoot, Williams paid less than $100.'
    USA Today. https://www.usatoday.com/story/life/people/
    2018/01/09/exclusive-wahlberg-paid-1-5-m-all-money-
    reshoot-williams-got-less-than-1-000/1018351001/.
    (Accessed July 7, 2023)
69. Busby, Nicole. 2018. 'The evolution of gender equality
    and related employment policies: The case of work–family
    reconciliation.' *International Journal of Discrimination and the
    Law.* vol. 18, nos. 2–3. https://journals.sagepub.com/
    doi/10.1177/1358229118788458. (Accessed July 7, 2023)
70. Dugarova, Esuna. 2020. 'Unpaid Care Work in Times of the
    Covid-19 Crisis.' *United Nations Development Program.* https://
    www.un.org/development/desa/family/wp-content/
    uploads/sites/23/2020/06/Unpaid-care-work-in-times-of-
    the-COVID-19-crisis.Duragova.pdf. (Accessed July 7, 2023)
71. 'The Global Childcare Workload From School and Preschool
    Closures During the COVID-19 Pandemic.' *Center for Global
    Development.* www.cgdev.org/publication/global-childcare-
    workload-school-and-preschool-closures-during-covid-19-
    pandemic. (Accessed July 7, 2023)
72. Coffrey, Clare, Patricia Espinoza Revollo, Rowan Harvey, Max
    Lawson, Anam Parvez Butt, Kim Piaget, Diana Sarosi, and

Julie Thekkudan. 2020. 'Time to Care: Unpaid and underpaid care work and the global inequality crisis.' *Oxfam.* https://oxfamilibrary.openrepository.com/handle/10546/620928. (Accessed July 7, 2023)

73. Feig, Christy. 2011. 'Exclusive breastfeeding for six months best for babies everywhere.' *World Health Organization.* https://www.who.int/news/item/15-01-2011-exclusive-breastfeeding-for-six-months-best-for-babies-everywhere. (Accessed July 7, 2023)

74. Runquist, Jennifer. 2007. 'Persevering Through Postpartum Fatigue.' *Journal of Obstetric, Gynecologist, & Neonatal Nursing.* vol. 36, no. 1. https://doi.org/10.1111/j.1552-6909.2006.00116.x. (Accessed July 7, 2023)

75. Poduval, Jayita, and Murali Poduval. 2009. 'Working mothers: how much working, how much mothers, and where is the womanhood?' *Mens Sana Monogr.* vol. 7, no. 1. https://www.ncbi.nlm.nih.gov/pmc/articles/PMC3151456/. (Accessed July 7, 2023)

76. Kanter, Rosabeth. 1999. 'Deloitte & Touche (A): A Hole in the Pipeline.' *Harvard Business School.* https://www.hbs.edu/faculty/Pages/item.aspx?num=375. (Accessed July 7, 2023)

77. 'The leaking pipeline: Where are our female leaders? 79 women share their stories.' *Global Human Capital.* https://www.pwc.com/gx/en/women-at-pwc/assets/leaking_pipeline.pdf. (Accessed July 7, 2023)

78. 'She Figures 2015 - Gender in Research and Innovation.' *Data Europa.* https://data.europa.eu/data/datasets/she-figures-2015-gender-in-research-and-innovation?locale=en. (Accessed July 7, 2023)

79. Ely, Robin, Pamela Stone, and Colleen Ammerman. 2014. 'Rethink What You "Know" About High-Achieving Women.' *Harvard Business Review.* https://hbr.org/2014/12/rethink-what-you-know-about-high-achieving-women. (Accessed July 7, 2023).

80. Refer to endnote 79.
81. 'Closing the Gender Gap: Act Now.' *Organisation for Economic Co-operation and Development.* http://dx.doi.org/10.1787/9789264179370-en. (Accessed July 7, 2023)
82. Refer to endnote 79.
83. Berman, Robby. 2018. 'Women are more productive than men, according to new research.' *World Economic Forum.* https://www.weforum.org/agenda/2018/10/women-are-more-productive-than-men-at-work-these-days. (Accessed July 7, 2023)
84. Coury, Sara, Jess Huang, Ankur Kumar, Sara Prince, Alexis Krivkovich, and Lareina Yee. 2020. 'Women in the Workplace 2020.' *McKinsey & Company.* https://www.mckinsey.com/featured-insights/diversity-and-inclusion/women-in-the-workplace. (Accessed July 7, 2023)
85. Viscussi, W. Kip. 1980. 'Sex Differences in Worker Quitting.' *Vanderbilt University Institutional Repository.* https://ir.vanderbilt.edu/handle/1803/6615. (Accessed July 7, 2023)
86. Refer to endnote 81.
87. '2016 NSCH Guide to Topics and Questions.' *Data Resource Center for Child and Adolescent Health.* www.childhealthdata.org/learn-about-the-nsch/topics_questions/2016-nsch-guide-to-topics-and-question. (Accessed July 7, 2023)
88. Kumari, K. Thriveni, and V. Rama Devi. 2013. 'Work-Life Balance of Women Employees—A Challenge for The Employee and The Employer In 21st Century.' *Pacific Business Review International.* http://dspace.cus.ac.in/jspui/handle/1/3914. (Accessed July 7, 2023)
89. Gamage, S. K., et al. 2019. 'Work Life Balance and Employee Retention: Experience of Women Employees in Leading Apparel Manufacturing . . .' *ResearchGate.* www.researchgate.net/publication/336412360_Work_Life_Balance_and_Employee_Retention_Experience_of_Women_Employees_in_Leading_Apparel_Manufacturing_Organization_in_Sri_Lanka. (Accessed July 7, 2023)

90. Refer to endnote 81.

91. Refer to endnote 34.

92. 'Women in Business and Management: Gaining momentum in Latin America and the Caribbean.' *International Labour Organization.* https://www.ilo.org/wcmsp5/groups/public/----ed_dialogue/---act_emp/documents/publication/wcms_579085.pdf. (Accessed July 7, 2023)

93. Bishop-Josef, Sandra, et al. 2018. 'Want to Grow the Economy? Fix the Child Care Crisis.' *Ready Nation.* https://strongnation.s3.amazonaws.com/documents/602/83bb2275-ce07-4d74-bcee-ff6178daf6bd.pdf. (Accessed July 7, 2023)

94. Brandon, Peter, and Jeromey Temple. 2016. 'Family Provisions at the Workplace and Their Relationship to Absenteeism, Retention, and Productivity of Workers: Timely Evidence from Prior Data.' *Wiley Online Library.* https://onlinelibrary.wiley.com/doi/abs/10.1002/j.1839-4655.2007.tb00071.x. (Accessed July 7, 2023)

95. Vanderkam, Laura. 2016. 'Why Offering Paid Maternity Leave Is Good For Business.' *Fast Company.* https://www.fastcompany.com/3064070/why-offering-paid-maternity-leave-is-good-for-business. (Accessed July 7, 2023)

96. Refer to endnote 77.

97. Kane, Libby. 2018. 'Sweden Is Apparently Full of "Latte Dads" Carrying Toddlers — and It's a Sign of Critical Social Change.' *Business Insider.* www.businessinsider.com/sweden-maternity-leave-paternity-leave-policies-latte-dads-2018-4. (Accessed July 7, 2023)

98. 'Employment: Time Spent in Paid and Unpaid Work, by Sex.' *Organisation for Economic Co-operation and Development.* https://stats.oecd.org/index.aspx?queryid=54757. (Accessed July 7, 2023)

99. Refer to endnote 97.

100. Smith, David G., and W. Brad Johnson. 2020. 'Gender Equity Starts in the Home.' *Harvard Business Review.* https://hbr.org/2020/05/gender-equity-starts-in-the-home. (Accessed July 7, 2023)

101. Wulfhorst, Ellen. 2019. 'Most men still don't take paternity leave, according to a new study.' *World Economic Forum.* https://www.weforum.org/agenda/2019/06/nappies-no-thanks-say-most-men-with-few-still-taking-full-paternity-leave. (Accessed July 7, 2023)

102. 'Report: 22 years until Swedish management teams are gender equal.' *The Local.* https://www.thelocal.se/20170911/report-22-years-until-swedish-management-teams-are-gender-equal/. (Accessed July 7, 2023)

103. 'Work–life Balance.' *Sweden Sverige.* https://sweden.se/life/society/work-life-balance. (Accessed July 7, 2023)

104. Gnewski, Madelaine. 2019. 'Sweden's Parental Leave May Be Generous, but It's Tying Women to the Home.' *The Guardian.* www.theguardian.com/commentisfree/2019/jul/10/sweden-parental-leave-corporate-pressure-men-work. (Accessed July 7, 2023)

105. Sinek, Simon. 2014. *Leaders Eat Last: Why Some Teams Pull Together and Others Don't.* Penguin Random House.

106. Tisdale, Sandee. 2012. 'Adolescent Well-being Outcomes of Parental Perceptions of Work: Effects of Family Processes.' *Boston College University Libraries.* https://dlib.bc.edu/islandora/object/bc-ir:101872/datastream/PDF/view. (Accessed July 7, 2023)

107. 'How Has the Number of Female CEOs in Fortune 500 Companies Changed Over the Last 20 Years?' *World Economic Forum.* www.weforum.org/agenda/2022/03/ceos-fortune-500-companies-female (Accessed July 7, 2023)

108. Refer to endnote 59.

109. Krapf, Matthias, Heinrich W. Ursprung, and Christian Zimmermann. 2014. 'Parenthood and Productivity of Highly Skilled Labor: Evidence from the Groves of Academe, Federal Reserve Bank of St. Louis.' *Economic Research, Federal Reserve Bank of St. Louis.* https://doi.org/10.20955/wp.2014.001. (Accessed July 7, 2023)

110. Ganley, Colleen. 2018. 'Are Boys Better Than Girls at Math?' *Scientific American.* https://www.scientificamerican.com/article/are-boys-better-than-girls-at-math/. (Accessed July 7, 2023); 'The Myth of the Male Math Brain.' *AUUW.* https://www.aauw.org/resources/article/the-myth-of-the-male-math-brain/. (Accessed July 7, 2023)

111. C.W. 2014. 'Proof that you should have a life.' *The Economist.* https://www.economist.com/free-exchange/2014/12/09/proof-that-you-should-get-a-life. (Accessed July 7, 2023)

112. 'Programming to the Extreme - the Relationship Between Hours Worked and Productivity.' *Stanford University.* https://cs.stanford.edu/people/eroberts/cs201/projects/crunchmode/econ-hours-productivity.html. (Accessed July 7, 2023)

113. 'Gender Insights Report How Women Find Jobs Differently.' *LinkedIn.* https://business.linkedin.com/content/dam/me/business/en-us/talent-solutions-lodestone/body/pdf/Gender-Insights-Report.pdf. (Accessed July 7, 2023)

114. Refer to endnote 113.

115. Ibarra, Herminia, Robin Ely, and Kolb Deborah. 2013. 'Women Rising: The Unseen Barriers.' *Harvard Business Review.* https://oae.illinois.edu/wp-content/uploads/2022/06/Women-Rising-The-Unseen-Barriers-Harvard-Business-Review-0913.pdf. (Accessed July 7, 2023)

116. MacBride, Katie. 2021. 'Imposter Syndrome: The One Vital Question Men Have to Ask Themselves.' *Inverse.*

www.inverse.com/mind-body/imposter-syndrome-one-question. (Accessed July 7, 2023)

117. Bravata, Dena M., Sharon A. Watts, Autumn L. Keefer et al. 2019. 'Prevalence, Predictors, and Treatment of Impostor Syndrome: A Systematic Review.' *Journal of General Internal Medicine*. vol. 35. https://link.springer.com/article/10.1007/s11606-019-05364-1. (Accessed August 7, 2023)

118. Refer to endnote 40

119. 'Language Log: Sex-linked Lexical Budgets.' *Language Log*. http://itre.cis.upenn.edu/~myl/languagelog/archives/003420.html. (Accessed July 7, 2023)

120. Mehl, Matthias R., Simine Vazire, Nairán Ramírez-Esparza, Richard Slatcher, James W. Pennebaker. 2007. 'Are Women Really More Talkative Than Men?' *ResearchGate*, https://www.researchgate.net/publication/6223260_Are_Women_Really_More_Talkative_Than_Men (Accessed August 7, 2023)

121. Balakrishnan, Anita. 2017. 'Uber Board Member — Who Helped Lead Sexism Investigation — Joked That Uber's Female Board Members Talk Too Much.' *CNBC*. https://www.cnbc.com/2017/06/13/uber-board-member-david-bonderman-sexist-comment-at-culture-meeting.html. (Accessed July 7, 2023)

122. Smith-Lovin, Lynn, and Charles Brody. 1989. 'Interruptions in Group Discussions: The Effects of Gender and Group Composition.' *American Sociological Review*. https://www.jstor.org/stable/2095614?seq=1#page_scan_tab_contents (Accessed 7 Jul. 2023)

123. Maranz, Felice, and Rebecca Greenfield. 2018. 'Men Get the First, Last and Every Other Word on Earnings Calls.' *Bloomberg*. https://www.bloomberg.com/news/articles/2018-09-13/men-get-the-first-last-and-every-other-word-on-earnings-calls. (Accessed July 7, 2023)

124. Karpowitz, Christopher F., et al. 2012. 'Gender Inequality in Deliberative Participation.' *American Political Science Review*. vol. 106, no. 3, pp. 533–47. https://doi.org/10.1017/s0003055412000329. (Accessed July 7, 2023)

125. Wodak, Ruth (ed.). 2017. 'Gender and Discourse.' *Sage Studies in Discourse*. https://time.com/wp-content/uploads/2017/06/d3375-genderandlanguageintheworkplace.pdf. (Accessed July 7, 2023)

126. 'Women speak less when they're outnumbered.' *Science Daily*. https://www.sciencedaily.com/releases/2012/09/12 0918121257.htm. (Accessed September 30, 2023)

There is an exception to this rule when there is unanimous instead of majority voting.

127. Karpowitz, Christopher, and Tali Mendelberg. 2014. *The Silent Sex: Gender, Deliberation and Institutions*. Princeton University Press.

128. Refer to endnote 127.

129. 'Women Don't Always Find Power in Numbers.' *Princeton University*. www.princeton.edu/news/2014/09/30/women-dont-always-find-power-numbers (Accessed July 6, 2023)

130. 'Women Face Backlash for Speaking up at Work.' *Association for Psychological Science*. www.psychologicalscience.org/news/minds-business/women-face-backlash-for-speaking-up-at-work.html. (Accessed July 7, 2023)

131. Brescoll, Victoria L. 2011. 'Who Takes the Floor and Why.' *Administrative Science Quarterly*. vol. 56, no. 4, pp. 622–41. https://doi.org/10.1177/0001839212439994. (Accessed July 7, 2023)

132. *Ban Bossy. Encourage Girls to Lead.* https://banbossy.com/. (Accessed July 7, 2023)

133. Subtirelu, Nic. 2014. 'No Really, Bossy Is Gendered.' *Linguistic Pulse*. www.linguisticpulse.com/2014/03/28/no-really-bossy-is-gendered. (Accessed July 7, 2023)

134. Roy, Jessica. 2014. 'I Don't Give a $*%& if You Call Me Bossy.' *Time*. www.time.com/21498/i-dont-give-a-if-you-call-me-bossy. (Accessed July 7, 2023)

135. Grant, Adam. 2014. 'Why Girls Get Called Bossy, and How to Avoid It.' *LinkedIn*. https://www.linkedin.com/pulse/20140316150417-69244073-why-girls-get-called-bossy-and-how-to-avoid-it

136. Clerkin, Cathleen, Christine A. Crumbacher, Julia Fernando, and William A. (Bill) Gentry. 2015. 'Bossy: What's Gender Got to Do with It?' *Center of Creative Leadership*. https://cclinnovation.org/wp-content/uploads/2020/02/bossy2.pdf. (Accessed August 7, 2023)

137. Sandberg, Sheryl, and Anna Maria Chávez. 2014. 'Sheryl Sandberg and Anna Maria Chávez on "Bossy", the Other B-word.' *The Wall Street Journal*. https://www.wsj.com/articles/sheryl-sandberg-and-anna-maria-chavez-on-bossy-the-other-b-word-1394236848. (Accessed August 7, 2023)

138. Kolhatkar, S. 2016. 'How Women Decide.' *The New York Times*. https://www.nytimes.com/2016/05/15/books/review/how-women-decide-by-therese-huston.html. (Accessed July 7, 2023)

139. 'What Makes a Good Leader, and Does Gender Matter?' *Pew Research Center*. www.pewresearch.org/social-trends/2015/01/14/chapter-2-what-makes-a-good-leader-and-does-gender-matter. (Accessed July 7, 2023)

140. Benko, Cathy. 2014. 'How Women Decide.' *Harvard Business Review*. https://hbr.org/2013/09/how-women-decide. (Accessed July 8, 2023)

141. Huston, Therese. 2016. *How Women Decide*. Houghton Mifflin Harcourt.

142. Delaney, Rebecca K., et al. 2015. 'Variations in Decision-making Profiles by Age and Gender: A Cluster-analytic

Approach.' *Personality and Individual Differences.* vol. 85, pp. 19–24. https://doi.org/10.1016/j.paid.2015.04.034. (Accessed July 8, 2023)

143. Reilly, David J., et al. 2022. 'Gender Differences in Self-Estimated Intelligence: Exploring the Male Hubris, Female Humility Problem.' *Frontiers in Psychology.* vol. 13, https://doi.org/10.3389/fpsyg.2022.812483. (Accessed July 8, 2023)

144. Bart, Chris, and Gregory McQueen. 2013. 'Why Women Make Better Directors.' *INDERSCIENCE Publishers.* www.inderscience.com/info/inarticle.php?artid=52743. (Accessed July 8, 2023)

145. 'Effective, Decisive, and Inclusive: Women's Leadership in COVID-19 Response and Recovery.' *UN Women.* www.unwomen.org/en/digital-library/publications/2021/10/effective-decisive-and-inclusive-womens-leadership-in-covid-19-response-and-recovery. (Accessed July 8, 2023)

146. Dreyer, Anna, et al. 'Risky Decision Making Under Stressful Conditions: Men and Women With Smaller Cortisol Elevations Make Riskier Social and Economic Decisions.' *Frontiers in Psychology.* vol. 13. https://doi.org/10.3389/fpsyg.2022.810031. (Accessed July 8, 2023)

147. In addition to Huston's description, here is the original article: https://www.ncbi.nlm.nih.gov/pmc/articles/PMC2698212/. This article refers to many other studies comparing gender, stress and risk taking—with similar conclusions. Lighthall, Nicole, Mara Mather, and Marissa A. Gorlik, 2019, 'Acute stress increases sex differences in risk seeking in the balloon analogue risk task.' *PubMed.* https://pubmed.ncbi.nlm.nih.gov/19568417/#:~:text=Methodology%2Fprincipal%20findings%3A%20In%20this%20study%2C%20participants%20played%20a,taking%20among%20men%20but%20decreased%20it%20among%20women. (Accessed August 7, 2023)

148. Nikolova, Hristina. 2016. 'Men Choose Differently When They Choose With Other Men.' *Harvard Business Review.* www.hbr.org/2016/09/men-choose-differently-when-they-choose-with-other-men. (Accessed July 8, 2023)

149. Dolan, Brian. 2023. 'Enron Executives: What Happened, and Where Are They Now?' *Investopedia.* www.investopedia.com/enron-executives-6831970. (Accessed July 8, 2023)

150. Shrira, Ilan. 2011. 'Women More Likely Than Men to See Nuance When Making Decisions.' *Scientific American.* www.scientificamerican.com/article/sex-roles-and-seeing-the-world-in-black-and-white. (Accessed July 8, 2023)

151. Meyer, Erin. 2014. *The Culture Map: Breaking Through the Invisible Boundaries of Global Business.* Hachette.

152. Refer to endnote 140.

153. Refer to endnote 40.

154. '"Everything I Have to Do is Tied to a Man" Women and Qatar's Male Guardianship Rules.' *Human Rights Watch.* https://www.hrw.org/report/2021/03/29/everything-i-have-do-tied-man/women-and-qatars-male-guardianship-rules#:~:text=Women%20must%20obtain%20permission%20from,jobs%2C%20and%20obtain%20some%20reproductive. (Accessed on September 30, 2023)

155. 'The Diversity and Inclusion Revolution: Eight Powerful Truths.' *Deloitte Insights.* https://www2.deloitte.com/us/en/insights/deloitte-review/issue-22/diversity-and-inclusion-at-work-eight-powerful-truths.html. (Accessed July 8, 2023)

156. Åkestam, Nina, Sara Rosengren, Micael Dahlén, Karina T. Liljedal, Hanna Berg. 2021. 'Gender stereotypes in advertising have negative cross-gender effects.' *Emerald Insight.* https://www.emerald.com/insight/content/doi/10.1108/EJM-02-2019-0125/full/html#sec015 (Accessed August 7, 2023)

157. n.a. 2021. 'Why Organizations Need More Women in Sales.' *St. Catherine University.* https://www.stkate.edu/

academics/women-in-leadership-degrees/women-in-sales
(Accessed August 7, 2023)

158. 'Women Are WAY Better Than Men at This High-value Sales
     Skill.' *Gong.* www.gong.io/resources/labs/women-are-way-
     better-than-men-at-this-high-value-sales-skill.   (Accessed
     July 8, 2023)

159. 'Advancing Women in the Workplace: How We Won the
     Catalyst Award 2021.' *Barilla.* www.barillagroup.com/en/
     stories/stories-list/catalyst-award-2021/. (Accessed July 8,
     2023)

160. Reuters. 2013. 'Pasta Baron Apologizes for Anti-gay
     Comments.' *CNBC.* www.cnbc.com/2013/09/27/pasta-
     baron-apologizes-for-anti-gay-comments.html. (Accessed July
     8, 2023)

161. Buckley, Thomas. 2019. 'Barilla Pasta's Turnaround
     From Homophobia to National Pride.' *Bloomberg.* www.
     bloomberg.com/news/features/2019-05-07/barilla-pasta-s-
     turnaround-from-homophobia-to-national-pride. (Accessed
     July 8, 2023)

162. 'Qatar World Cup Ambassador Says Homosexuality Is
     "Damage in the Mind."' *Reuters.* www.reuters.com/lifestyle/
     sports/qatar-world-cup-ambassador-says-homosexuality-is-
     damage-mind-2022-11-08. (Accessed July 8, 2023)

163. Gowar, Rex. 2010. 'Blatter Apologises for Remarks
     About Gay Fans.' *Reuters.* www.reuters.com/article/idIN
     India-53640020101217. (Accessed July 8, 2023)

164. 'Closing Gender Pay Gaps Is More Important Than Ever.'
     UN News. https://news.un.org/en/story/2022/09/1126901
     (Accessed July 8, 2023)

165. 'The Proportion of Female Doctors Has Increased in All
     OECD Countries over the past Two Decades.' *Organisation for
     Economic Co-operation and Development.* www.oecd.org/gender/

data/the-proportion-of-female-doctors-has-increased-in-all-oecd-countries-over-the-past-two-decades.htm. (Accessed July 8, 2023)

166. Franks, Suzanne. 2011. 'Attitudes to Women in the BBC in the 1970s – Not so Much a Glass Ceiling as One of Reinforced Concrete.' *Westminster Papers in Communication and Culture*. vol. 8, no. 3, p. 123. https://doi.org/10.16997/wpcc.136. (Accessed July 8, 2023)

167. Edmondson, Amy C. 2019. *The Fearless Organization: Creating Psychological Safety in the Workplace for Learning, Innovation, and Growth*. Wiley.

168. Accredited to Dr. Rod Napier by some sources: https://www.tarleton.edu/strategicplan/documents/leadershipdocs/The_20-60-20_Rule.pdf

169. Wakefield, Jane. 2021. 'The tech billionaire who is putting women first.' *BBC News*. https://www.bbc.com/news/technology-56662100. (Accessed July 8, 2023)

170. Au-Yeung, Angel. 2021. 'Bumble Cofounder Becomes World's Youngest Self-Made Woman Billionaire, Thanks to IPO.' *Forbes*. https://www.forbes.com/sites/angelauyeung/2021/02/11/bumble-founder-whitney-wolfe-herds-fortune-rockets-past-1-billion-as-dating-app-goes-public/?sh=909df1a578d9. (Accessed July 8, 2023)

171. 'Speciesism and the Idea of Equality.' 2009. *Cambridge University Press*. https://www.cambridge.org/core/journals/philosophy/article/abs/speciesism-and-the-idea-of-equality/89C0A6DD4548DFB68B5C67E227A3A16A. (Accessed July 8, 2023)

172. 'Understanding the Stress Response.' *Harvard Health*. www.health.harvard.edu/staying-healthy/understanding-the-stress-response. (Accessed July 8, 2023)

173. Psychiatric Medical Care Communications Team. 'The Difference Between Empathy and Sympathy.' *Psychiatric Medical Care.* www.psychmc.com/blogs/empathy-vs-sympathy (Accessed July 8, 2023)

174. See for instance, https://www.psychologytoday.com/sg/blog/the-well-being-toolkit/201909/beyond-empathy-the-power-compassion: 'Compassion goes further [than empathy] and involves a genuine wish or act to alleviate another's suffering and to be with another in their suffering.' Kurland, Beth. 2019. 'Beyond Empathy: The Power of Compassion.' *Psychology Today.*

175. Brooks, Alison Wood. 2023. 'How to Ask Great Questions.' *Harvard Business Review.* https://www.hbs.edu/faculty/Pages/item.aspx?num=54500. (Accessed July 8, 2023)

176. Cialdini, Robert B. 2007. *Influence: The Psychology of Persuasion.* Collins.

177. Morris, B.S., Chrysochou, P., Christensen, J.D. et al. 2019. Stories vs. facts: triggering emotion and action-taking on climate change. *Climatic Change.* vol. 154, 19–36. https://doi.org/10.1007/s10584-019-02425-6. (Accessed September 30, 2023)

178. Ibid.

179. Women's Leadership Lab Stanford University. 'Harnessing the Power of Stories [Video].' YouTube. https://youtu.be/oB7FfKPMZvw. (Accessed July 8, 2023)

180. Rev. Martin Luther King Jr. 'I Have a Dream.' 1963. *The Gilder Lehrman Institute of American History.*

181. Ely, Robin, Pamela Stone, and Colleen Ammerman. 2015. 'Rethink What You "Know" About High-Achieving Women.' *Harvard Business Review.* https://hbr.org/2014/12/rethink-what-you-know-about-high-achieving-women. (Accessed July 8, 2023)

182. 'Strategy and Goals.' *Unilever*. www.unilever.com/planet-and-society/equity-diversity-and-inclusion/strategy-and-goals. (Accessed July 8, 2023)

183. McIntyre, Lindsay-Rae. 2022. '2022 Diversity and Inclusion Report: Driving Progress Through Greater Accountability and Transparency.' *The Official Microsoft Blog*. https://blogs.microsoft.com/blog/2022/10/27/2022-diversity-inclusion-report-driving-progress-through-greater-accountability-and-transparency/. (Accessed July 8, 2023)

184. 'Microsoft's 2021 Diversity and Inclusion Report: Demonstrating Progress and Remaining Accountable to Our Commitments.' *The Official Microsoft Blog*. https://blogs.microsoft.com/blog/2021/10/20/microsofts-2021-diversity-inclusion-report-demonstrating-progress-and-remaining-accountable-to-our-commitments/. (Accessed July 8, 2023)

185. MetaMind Training. 'Communicating With Impact [Video].' YouTube. www.youtube.com/watch?v=3_FHvMHN45U. (Accessed July 8, 2023)

186. Gilchrist, Karen. 2019. 'Indra Nooyi Has Advice for Stamping Out Workplace Bias.' *CNBC*. www.cnbc.com/2019/09/26/ex-pepsico-ceo-indra-nooyi-has-advice-for-stamping-out-workplace-bias.html. (Accessed July 8, 2023)

187. Reuters. 2021. 'Don't be silent: How a 22-year-old woman helped bring down the Tokyo Olympics chief.' *CNN Sports*. https://edition.cnn.com/2021/02/18/sport/momoko-nojo-tokyo-olympics-spt-intl/index.html. (Accessed July 8, 2023)

188. Maruyama, Rikako. 2021. 'Japan Activist Welcomes Olympic Chief Resignation, but Says Sexism Much Wider.' *Reuters*. www.reuters.com/article/us-olympics-2020-mori-petition-idUSKBN2AC1BC. (Accessed July 8, 2023)

189. Rourke, Alison. 2012. 'Julia Gillard's Attack on Sexism Hailed as Turning Point for Australian Women.' *The Guardian.* https://www.theguardian.com/world/2012/oct/12/julia-gillard-sexism-australian-women. (Accessed July 8, 2023)

190. Refer to endnote 189.

191. 'Five Fifty.' *McKinsey & Company.* https://www.mckinsey.com/featured-insights/leadership/five-fifty-is-it-safe. (Accessed July 8, 2023)